mystifying recommending delighting repr... imagining visualizing experiencing marking forcing keeping standing listening yielding crossing marking building transforming seeing scaling keeping yielding enchanting editing inventing producing talking preparing navigating examining reflecting communicating embracing inspiring connecting enchanting satisfying starting acknowledging enjoying

designing:

Ivan Chermayeff
Tom Geismar
Steff Geissbuhler

designing**:**

 Published by Graphis Inc.

Published by
Graphis Inc.
307 Fifth Avenue
New York, New York 10016

©2003 Chermayeff & Geismar Inc.

Printed and bound in Italy
Bolis Poligrafiche

This book is typeset in Franklin Gothic

The paper is Scheufelen
150 gsm PhoeniXmotion Xenon

Library of Congress Control Number:
2003108050

ISBN: 1-932026-14-2

Acknowledgments

This book would not have come to fruition without the help of many individuals to whom we are deeply indebted:

Emanuela Frigerio, a principal of the firm, who immersed herself in our archives, made the selections of images, found connections, and designed the pages with flair.

Paul Rosenthal, who expressed our thoughts for the chapter introductions and brilliantly edited our text.

James Harrison, who went well beyond proofreading with his incisive editorial observations and suggestions.

Juanita Dugdale, who helped us early on with the concept and structure of the book.

Our staff, especially Michele Miller and Gabriele Schies for translating the images and design of the book into digital files.

Jack Masey and Rusty Russell, our original partners in MetaForm with whom we design major exhibitions.

John Hockenberry, for his thoughtful introduction, and Martin Pedersen, the publisher of Graphis Press, for his input and support.

Finally, our partners Keith Helmetag, Jonathan Alger, Herman Eberhardt and Emanuela Frigerio, who have contributed so much to the work; to John Grady, who was our partner for many years; and to Robert Brownjohn, who was with us at the start of this journey.

Of demons, dancing, and designing
John Hockenberry

To attempt to write the foreword for a book on designing is already to commit the sin of being extraneous in the presence of authors and readers who have spent as much time erasing and deleting as they have creating. If there is anything I have learned in my lifetime in the world of design, it is that design is best left to designers. This presupposes, however, that anyone else is clamoring to do design, a dubious assumption.

In our age there is a sense that design is flourishing, that in a world awash with competing symbols of culture and nationalism, the commercial and the sacred, it is perhaps only the sensibility of design that can mediate between the poles of meaning and noise. But design in the United States remains something of an untrustworthy outsider, more cuisine than essential nutrition. Aside from the fashion world's seductive portrayal of designer as the celebrity's celebrity, designers toil in obscurity, performing their quiet magic.

Successful design seeks concealed meanings and makes them unforgettable. Design is the geology of language, it continually traces the skyline of a civilization finding new forms and emblems of the mark humanity has left on this planet. But truly, attempting to describe design is most like tap dancing across a gymnasium floor covered in ball bearings. No designer will ever accept a single metaphor as descriptive of what he or she does, instead greeting offerings with a gentle squint and slightly cocked head and a polite but dismissive, "That's not quite it."

The best designers — and the work of some of the very best can be found in these pages — embody a passionate belief that text and symbols are the seeds for crystals of meaning that can always be refined and enlarged. Design is certainly among civilization's few truly benign obsessions. Perhaps a CAT scan might find in the brains of great designers the elegant signature of their demons in the form of some mild mental illness.

Designers have never enslaved people, never lusted for power. There are no operas about consumptive designers who starved themselves and their families to produce portfolios of misunderstood typography. It is the rare designer who would even consider slicing off his or her ear (the asymmetry alone would no doubt hurt more than the wound). But designers retain an enormous emotional commitment to the precision and exactitude of images that are largely disposable.

In the disconnected fleeting punctuation of causes, corporate campaigns, pamphlets (glossy and not), exhibits, and curricula, the story line of designers' work over time gets lost. Strung together across the numerous jobs and client specifications, design becomes a search for truth and a devotion to theme and meaning. Most important, design celebrates reverence for the unexpected truth, for meanings lost and found. With a passion for the obscure, designers seek the universal. And it is about at this point that the ball bearings send my tap shoes in different directions and I hit the hard floor. "Thanks, but that's not quite it."

As a child I asked my dad what he did at work. His answer was always, "I'm a designer." To this day my definition of what he does is sub-verbal. It is the image of him sitting in his exotic-looking chair sketching and erasing while listening to opera on the radio. It is the same with every designer I have ever met. Some do their sketches in the mind, some on computer; few listen to opera these days but little else has changed from those magical days in my father's basement office.

If I have retained anything else from those days it is that design is best left to designers.

As we would not leave plumbing, piloting, or heart surgery to walk-on practitioners, design demands a certain ineffable genius to achieve anything of value. But then you've probably already stopped reading these words long ago and turned the pages as any designer would, avoiding the extraneous, to seek the essential meaning within. Design ought to need no captioning. A good design is worth a thousand pictures. There are about that many in this book.

Beginning with words:

Finding metaphors:

Commenting:

Telling stories:

Avoiding the obvious:

Reinterpreting the familiar:

Demystifying data:

Expressing personality:

Teaching through play:

Delighting audiences:

Gathering and collecting:

Shifting scale:

Taking artistic license:

Repeating, repeating:

Realizing ideas:

Guiding the way:

Marking passages:

Creating landmarks:

Representing the nation:

Passing time:

Expressing ideas typographically 10

Expressing a concept visually 34

Giving a voice to points of view 52

Making history come alive 66

Confounding expectations 84

Celebrating nature 102

Explaining abstract concepts 124

Crafting a visual identity 138

Creating playful, interactive learning experiences 160

Building audience anticipation 172

Transforming the ordinary into the extraordinary 186

Manipulating size to attract attention 210

Erasing the line between art and design 224

Creating more than the sum of its parts 242

Sparking instant understanding 258

Pinpointing destinations with visual prompts 270

Celebrating events and rites of passage 286

Making places memorable 300

Finding new expressions of familiar symbols 316

Designing over four decades 332

Beginning with words
Expressing ideas typographically

Designers communicate with form, color, images, and composition. Writers communicate with words. When the two work in tandem, they are a powerful team. Finding visual possibilities within the text combines the art of language with the language of art. The result is an added layer of meaning and nuance that neither medium can easily convey on its own. Fundamentally, graphic design is about presenting the printed word. So, in a sense, tinkering with typography is just returning to our roots—and giving those roots a playful twist.

Cherm Steff & Geissbuhler

A picture is worth 1,000 words. (Probably more by now, adjusted for inflation.) But what about a picture made of words?

For a 2001 lecture on "collaboration" at the Portfolio Center in Atlanta, type is used to draw a very different picture. Here, teamwork takes visual form thanks to a happy discovery: that the beginning and end of partner Steff Geissbuhler's name has seven letters in common with the end and beginning of the names of his colleagues.

A poster for the Simpson Paper Company, part of a series on "Connections," draws a picture with type of the provocative connection between us and our "intelligent" machines. The letters R-O-B-O-T-I-C form a classic toy robot, an anthro-pomorphic machine fashioned from that uniquely human achievement: language. To emphasize the underlying tension between automation and creativity, the robot's antenna is a question mark.

THE FIRST NEW YORK INTERNATIONAL FESTIVAL OF THE ARTS JUNE 13 - JULY 11 1988

MUSIC, DANCE, THEATRE, OPERA, AND FILM
OF THE 20TH CENTURY

History teaches that writing began with pictograms— drawings that represent objects or ideas. Over time, these grew gradually more abstract and stylized, eventually becoming letterforms.

This poster for the New York International Festival of the Arts brings the process full circle, using pictures to represent ideas *and* letterforms. A treble clef becomes an "S" and a Manhattan skyscraper an "I," blurring the boundary between text and illustration. It's a lively hybrid that suggests the vitality of a festival as well as the fresh approach and theatricality one expects from the arts.

The Guggenheim and Whitney museums in New York City were built to present works of art. But sometimes, the messenger becomes more notable than the message. Both museums are high-profile personalities in their own right; readily recognizable landmarks whose distinctive buildings are often as well known as the works they display.

In one poster, the Guggenheim name morphs into Frank Lloyd Wright's distinctive building facade. In the other, the stepped type for the Whitney echoes the architecture of Marcel Breuer's inverted ziggurat.

Letters create an aura as well as words.

A cover collage for the eighth issue of Mexico's leading design magazine plays with the publication's bilingualism. The two languages dance together in a tango of type, "ocho" and "eight" entwined in a cross-cultural dialogue.

An annual report cover for Aiken Industries pushes type tightly together to evoke quite a different mood. The bold, angular slab-serif type allows the letters to fit together snugly—a strong, stable, solid presence. The company name, broken into three lines of alternately positive and negative letters, shifts the visual emphasis to an interesting mix of seemingly abstract forms.

Aiken Industries, Inc.

Annual Report 1969

The Third Year

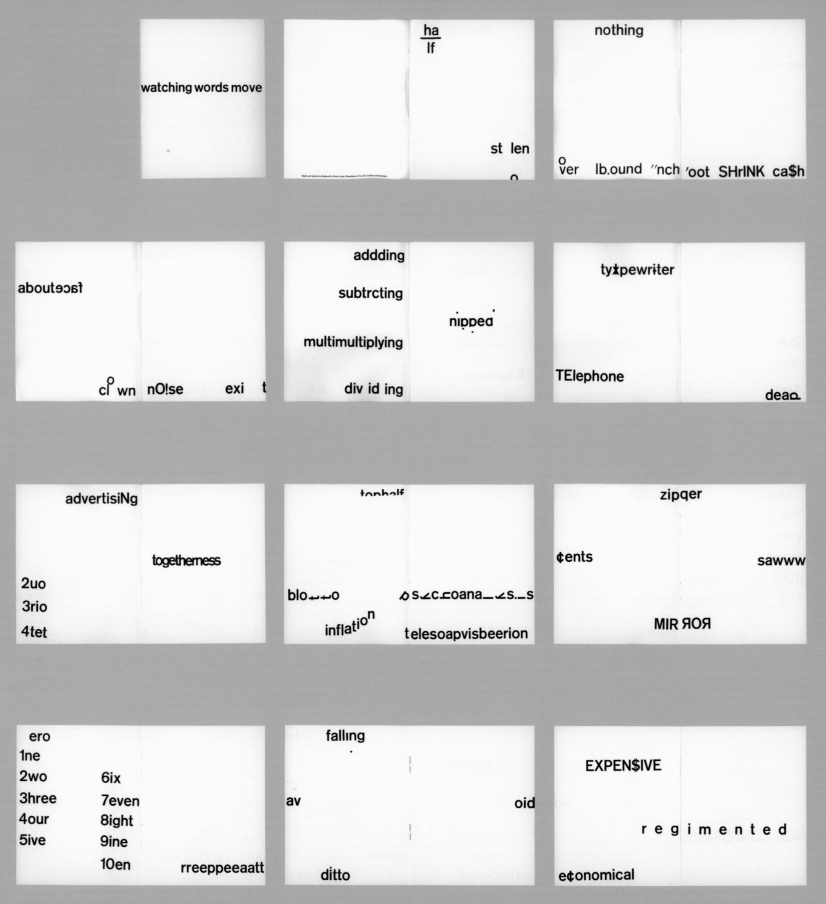

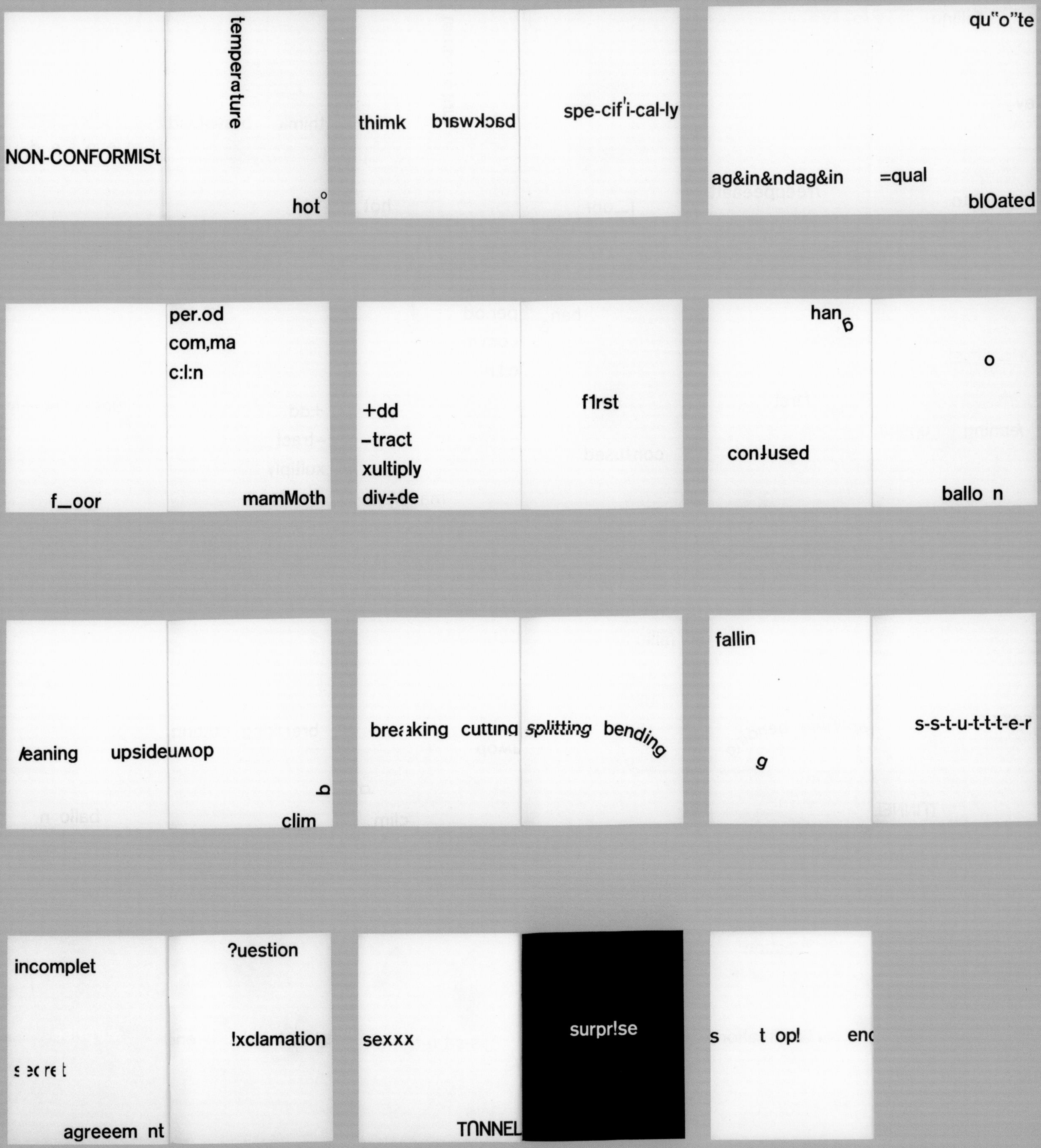

NON-CONFORMISt

temperature

hot°

thimk   backward   spe-cif'i-cal-ly

qu"o"te

ag&in&ndag&in   =qual

blOated

per.od
com,ma
c:l:n

f_oor   mamMoth

+dd
−tract
xultiply
div÷de

f1rst

han_g

confused

o

ballo n

leaning   upsideuɯop

b

clim

breaking cutting *splitting* bending

fallin

g

s-s-t-u-t-t-t-e-r

incomplet   ?uestion

!xclamation

secret

agreeem nt

sexxx

TUNNEL

surpr!se

s   t op!   end

The Missile Mess

Show and tell. Words can do both simultaneously, communicating more forcefully as a result. When letters spell out words, they *tell* you something. But when they also act out on the page, they *show* the message.

A 1959 experimental type booklet, shown on the previous spread, uses letters to depict the actions that the words describe.

The same principle of "watching words move" is used dramatically in a *Harper's Magazine* cover highlighting "the missile mess." Here, the "i's" in "missile" have gone ballistic, launching their dots.

For Champion Papers, one of a series of 26 posters continues a long tradition of illuminated alphabets, using type to evoke the feeling of a word. It's a technique you can see in the newspaper every summer, as headlines encrusted with frost announce air conditioner sales. Here, an "F" blazes like those two inflammatory "f" words, "fire" and "flame."

Taking
Things
Apart
and
Putting
Things
Together

what chemistry is
what chemists do
and what the results
have been

sponsored by the
American Chemical
Society
on the occasion
of its 100th
anniversary

Union Carbide
270 Park Ave.
New York, N.Y. 10017

April 5-May 28, 1976
9:30-4:30 weekdays
Closed April 16,17
and Sundays
Admission: free

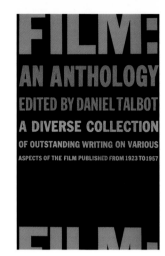

FILM:
AN ANTHOLOGY
EDITED BY DANIEL TALBOT
A DIVERSE COLLECTION
OF OUTSTANDING WRITING ON VARIOUS
ASPECTS OF THE FILM PUBLISHED FROM 1923 TO 1957
FILM:

Design is about communication.
Communication is about ideas.
Expressing ideas through
both words *and* graphics offers
an eloquent one-two punch.

A poster for a traveling exhibition sponsored by the American
Chemical Society uses this
approach to express the simple
fact that everything is made
of chemicals. The exhibition
title—"Taking Things Apart
and Putting Things Together"—
introduces the premise of
chemicals as building blocks.
Taking apart the words letter
by letter reveals the chemical
symbols lurking within.

A collection of film essays
employs a subtle form of
graphic play. The word "film" is
cropped along the top and
bottom of the cover to suggest
the movement of the film
as it sandwiches the subtitle
and author's name.

Ta K In g
Th In g S
Tartalum Indium
Potassium Indium
t H
A Pa R t
A Nd
Hydrogen
Protactinium Neodymium
Pu tt In g
Plutonium Indium
Th In g S
to Ge Th Er
Thorium Indium
Oxygen
Sulfur
Germanium
Thorium Erbium

Design: Chermayeff & Geismar Associates

A trio of book jackets illustrates visual wordplay with visual puns. The title of *The Unfinished Country* remains unfinished. For *The Age of Overkill*, words bleed off beyond the margins, while replacing letters with exclamation points dramatizes *The Art of Dramatic Writing*.

MAX LERNER

THE UNFINISHED COUNTRY

A BOOK OF AMERICAN SYMBOLS
BY THE AUTHOR OF
AMERICA AS A CIVILIZATION

THE AGE OF OVERKILL

A Preface to
World Politics
Max Lerner
author of AMERICA AS A CIVILIZATION

The Art of Dramat!c Wr!t!ng

Its Basis in the Creative Interpretation of Human Motives

Lajos Egri

Simon and Schuster $1.75

ACROBATS ASTROLOGERS
JUGGLERS FREAKS CLOWNS
ESCAPE ARTISTS VIOLINISTS
GROK GRAPES GRASS
UPS DOWNS SIDEWAYS
AIR-CONDITIONED
IN MORE WAYS THAN ONE
THE ULTIMATE LEGAL
ENTERTAINMENT EXPERIENCE

THE ELECTRIC CIRCUS
OPENS JUNE 28, 1967
23 ST. MARK'S PLACE, N.Y.C.
EAST VILLAGE
THINK ABOUT IT

A nonrepresentational painting can express feelings, arouse sensibilities, and convey meaning beyond any literal forms and figures. Similarly, designers can use typography in a more impressionistic way to convey the message, but go beyond the actual words on paper.

In the 1960s, the Electric Circus was the first of a new breed of multimedia nightclubs. The poster announcing its debut uses a double image of the type to capture in print the club's spark and novelty—the voltage and the showmanship embodied in the words "electric" and "circus."

Quite a different technique—a labor-intensive assemblage of overlapping, individually colored type—also creates an impression that expands on the written text. Here, a detail of a poster for the American Institute of Graphic Arts illustrates the broad scope of the organization's competitions and exhibitions. Lining up the type flush right spotlights the word "design" that unites the list.

National ♪ymphony

Letterforms, words, and typography are instruments to make graphic music, as demonstrated in this series of 1950s designs.

The initials of the Newport Jazz Festival suggest a road map when joined together, and inspired a highway sign to be placed within the "J," directing jazz lovers to Newport, Rhode Island.

The logo for the National Symphony employs color to say "national," and, to symbolize music, a treble clef replaces the "S" in "symphony."

Just as an orchestra unites distinct elements, keeping their individuality while working in concert, the sculptural wood type embraces distinct shapes to form a harmonious whole.

A folder for the Quartetto Italiano uses four vertical lines of text to symbolize both the four members of the string quartet *and* the strings of their instruments. A single line of text repeated and overprinted mimics the real-world vibrations of the strings.

The Quartetto Italiano

"The finest String Quartet, unquestionably, that our century has known," — New York Herald Tribune
"The finest String Quartet, unquestionably, that our century has known," — New York Herald Tribune
"The finest String Quartet, unquestionably, that our century has known," — New York Herald Tribune
"The finest String Quartet, unquestionably, that our century has known," — New York Herald Tribune

Type and letterforms can be tools to create an environment and capture a feeling.

At the 1958 World's Fair in Brussels, fragments of street signs, billboards, 24-sheet posters, and snippets of store-fronts created the feel of an American streetscape.

At the U.S. Pavilion at Expo '67 in Montreal, the jargon of the space program and the illuminated names of astronauts cover the outside of a ring enclosing a multiscreen presentation. As the words flash on and off, a moving presence is established.

For a Smithsonian Institution exhibit intended to present a clear explanation of "productivity," entering visitors are bombarded with a visual cacophony of economists' buzz-words back-projected onto the walls of a tunnel through which they must pass. Contrasted to this, what follows in the main body of the exhibition are analogies that get away from the usual techno-speak and convey, clearly and dramatically, the basic concept of productivity and its importance.

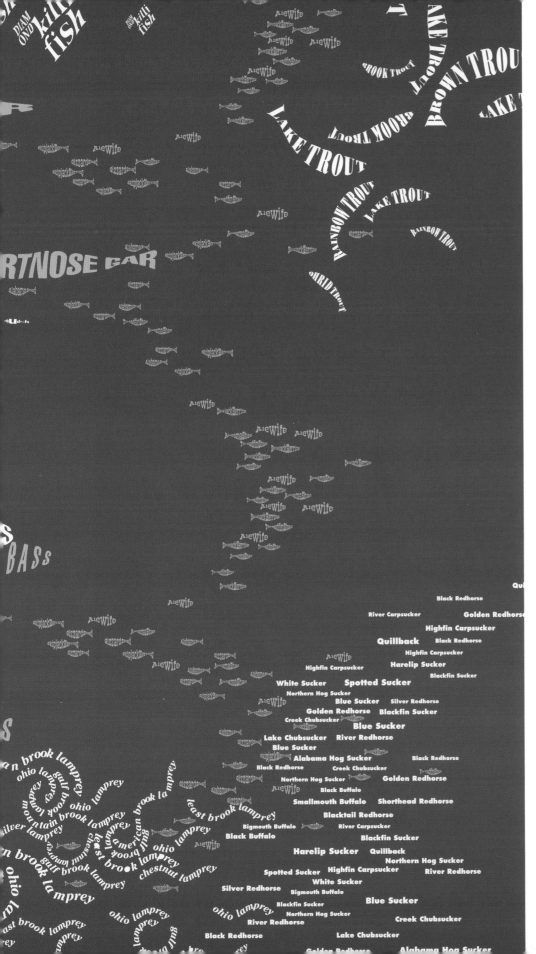

The word "type" derives from a Greek root meaning "to strike, or beat." For centuries, type was carved from wood or struck from metal, locked in a chase, and put in a press. This made it physically daunting to mix sizes or vary positions. Then computers came along. With the click of a mouse, Bodoni becomes Futura, fonts shrink or grow, and lines dance across the page.

At the Tennessee Aquarium, a 60-foot-high mural takes advantage of this flexibility. The state's waterways teem with an almost unparalleled variety of freshwater fish. Here, font diversity reflects species diversity, and fish names swim and leap and wriggle through a graphic waterway.

Computers are not the designer's only technological tool. Cameras too let us experiment with type. "Nature," heralded an exhibition of local artists addressing natural themes. To create this pro bono poster, natural materials were collected from a forest and turned into letterforms and photographed, creating a visually evocative font.

Letters can be drawn, type-styles selected and modified (sometimes dramatically), and words manipulated, all to enhance their meaning.

For a quarterly publication, *World Policy Journal*, the happy coincidence that "o" is the second letter of all three words inspired a logotype that replaced the letter with a solid dot. This dot then repeats down the page as a series of bullet points highlighting featured articles.

In a similar vein, the cover of *The Journal of Literary Translation* picks out letters that gradually "translate" into other words.

Banners for American Express Life Insurance, part of a motivational campaign for employees, highlight the shapes and patterns of the letters to infuse a simple, even mundane phrase with a flash of visual interest.

An *Atlantic Monthly* cover, spotlighting a lead article on race relations, uses an assemblage of found letters to dramatize the topic. The edgy tension of the "mismatched" forms and colors, apparently hastily juxtaposed and taped and pinned in place, hints at the pressures and instabilities roiling a diverse community.

Volume XIII, No3, Fall 1996 $7.50

WORLD POLICY JOURNAL

The Rise of "Lite" Powers
Barry Buzan and Gerald Segal

The Protestant Ethic   *Daniel Bell*
Unpackaging the Environment   *Kenneth H. Keller*

Hamilton's Way   *Walter Russell Mead*
The Tragedy of Isolationism   *Benjamin Schwarz*

The Next Mexican Revolution   *Andrew Reding*
Democracy Comes to Hispaniola   *Michele Wucker*

Controlling Global Finance   *Fred Block*
Socialism Reconsidered   *Norman Birnbaum*

India
Multicultural Democracy at the Millennium
Mira Kamdar

Workers of the World
Sebastião Salgado

TRANSLATION
TRANSLATION
TRANSLATION
AN LATI
I
I
S
S
S
S
ITALIAN
ISSUE

*The Journal of Literary Translation
Volume VIII, Winter 1981*

Fast and direct is not always the best way to communicate. Sometimes a more complex presentation slows down the reader, but allows for a richer understanding.

The overlapping numerals 1 to 5 were used on the cover of an IBM furniture standards manual to represent its five distinct sections.

A font of fanciful images and shapes spells out the title of a boxed set of multi-media disks produced by IBM. The result is a complex tapestry of associations and hidden meanings that readers must work at comprehending. They are rewarded with a rich and surprising array of implications and connections lurking below the surface text.

An advertisement sponsored by the Container Corporation of America also draws on reader associations to embellish its message, but in a very different way. Here, an Oliver Wendell Holmes quotation is rendered, line by line, in a procession of styles, moving from a child's scrawl to a more adult script, to a typewriter, to typeset Bodoni, to a more modern sans serif face, and finally to a font based on electronically readable type. Visually, Holmes' observation about new ideas becomes a microcosm of that concept— the procession from child to computer; from old to new.

MAN's mind,
stretched to
a new idea,
never goes back
to its original
DIMENSION.

Finding metaphors
Expressing a concept visually

Design is like writing—communicating ideas through forms instead of words. That sentence makes an analogy. It uses a commonplace activity (writing) to explain a less commonplace activity (designing). We often rely on analogy, and its cousins metaphor and simile, to mediate new experiences. They help us absorb unfamiliar information and confounding concepts. A metaphor can become like an interpreter, translating ideas into a language we can understand (to make a metaphor metaphor).

Design too can use these communication tools, using images or symbols or even colors in place of words, as in a rebus. But they also can do much more by representing complex concepts or triggering connections and emotions.

Metaphorical images communicate. Words communicate. Combining the two can double a design's effectiveness, evoking a range of emotions and ideas, as in these two posters for Mobil Masterpiece Theater.

The dove is a symbol of peace; cannonballs are a symbol of war. One sitting on the other joins the two rivals together, at least for a moment. The viewer both reads and perceives "war and peace."

Placing the homburg hat of diplomacy between the helmets of war restates the title wordlessly. The differing helmet styles of the doughboy and GI also summon a specific historical era, prompting an array of associations about the period from 1918 to 1939.

A dramatization of the Tolstoy novel presented on PBS-TV

Beginning November 20 Made possible by matching grants from

National Endowment for the Humanities & Mobil Oil Corporation

WAR AND PEACE

BETWEEN

THE WARS

To see it is to say it.

Using an actual butterfly instead of the word "butterfly" is memorable, simple, direct, and cannot be mistaken or misread. The "M" alone, of course, leaves the gender ambiguous, symbolizing the uncertainty of the play's main character. This poster for the Broadway production at the Longacre Theatre fashioned the butterfly from metallic foil to establish the elusive quality of the insect—and the character in the play. The foil reflects the light, shifting as the viewer moves.

A glove can be a symbol for hands, protection, particular kinds of work, elegance, fashion, or status. Consider the difference between a policeman stopping traffic with a white-gloved hand, or a medieval knight tossing his gauntlet at the feet of a foe. Or a worn-out and mangled worker's glove found on the street compared to the slinky, silky black glove of a fashion model. Gloves bring a range of possibilities, and associations. Hands, meanwhile, are a most expressive symbol for gestures. It only takes two white-gloved hands for us to fill in the blanks and visualize the Minstrel Man. On this bus shelter poster, the gloves are actual size, connecting the gesture with waiting bus riders standing in front of it.

The image above is the cover of a proposal to hold the Olympic Games in New York City. The arm of the Statue of Liberty does double duty as a signifier of the city and as an Olympic torchbearer.

Mobil Showcase presents

Minstrel Man

March 2   CBS channel 2   9pm

Mobil®

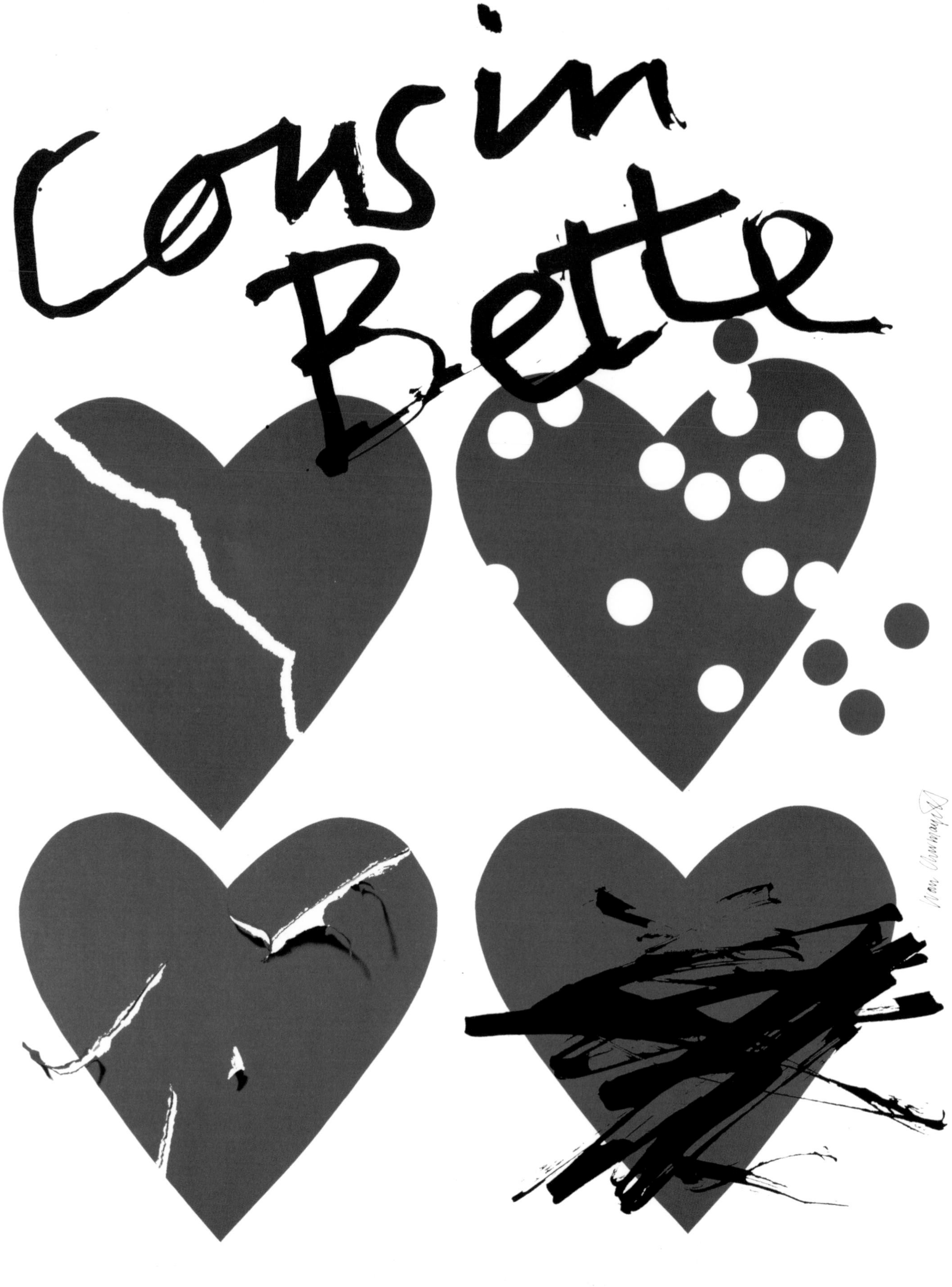
Cousin
Bette

There's no need to reinvent the wheel (though maybe it's time to reinvent that cliché about reinvention). As designers, we freely take advantage of popular metaphors, using their well-established symbolism as a foundation on which to build. The trick is to do what conventional wisdom says can't be done: to teach an old cliché new tricks—nurture new connotations and reappropriate the meaning rather than simply repeating the formula.

For *Cousin Bette*, who murdered her relatives, four tortured hearts suggest a life full of heartbreak, torn love affairs, hearts ripped apart, and murder.

As a case in point, consider that old graphic warhorse, the heart. For Cable Health Network, the addition of two green leaves transforms it into an apple, adding the idea of physical health to the notion of emotional health symbolized by the heart.

For the book cover for *The Wisdom of the Heart*, the heart symbol replaces the mind. A broken heart made out of concrete represents *The Livable City*, embodying both the love and the loss of the title.

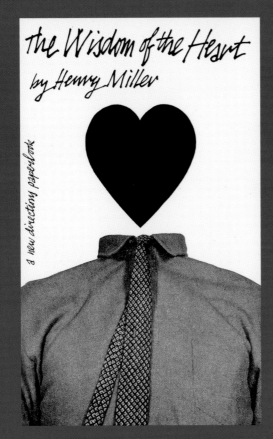

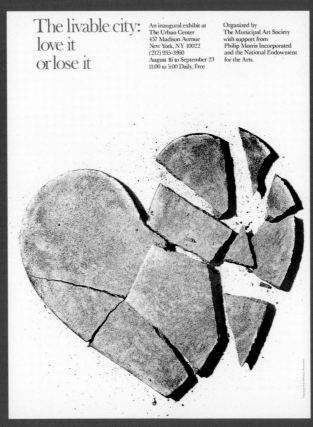

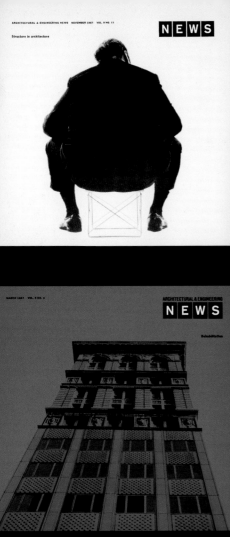

One of the more difficult things in designing a monthly magazine is reinterpreting a theme over and over again, finding ways to see the same topic from different perspectives. Several issues of *Architectural and Engineering News* use familiar imagery in seemingly unrelated juxtapositions to make each month's entry new and interesting.

On the theme of *Structure in architecture*, for example, a very light truss chair holds a very fat man. A rhino on top of a brick wall exemplifies the strength of materials. In another issue, a stethoscope takes the pulse of a medical facility. A high-rise office building with a floor as a drawer turns the building into a filing cabinet. Gingerbread pieces become building components to represent prefabrication. For an issue on *Building codes*, a structure of matchboxes goes up in flames. Tearing the skin off a building reveals its inner framework while an architect's compass is the needle on an LP record to suggest building acoustics.

FORTUNE

July 1963

5 0 0

Fortune's Directory of the Biggest Industrials

Japan's Hope—Business;   Taiwan's Muscle;   Red China's Economic Failure

Symbols are a sophisticated visual language, a code through which we add meaning and layers of associations. All around us we see symbols or metaphors that express a specific idea or whole concepts more effectively than any words. They are a form of visual shorthand for entire stories and complex associations. They allow us to tap an individual's vast visual experience in order to make new connections.

A *Fortune* magazine cover, for an issue listing the top 500 industrial corporations of the year, harnesses several metaphors. Combining the magazine's logo with a coarsely stenciled "500" and putting both against a piece of riveted steel lends a visceral sense of solidity and power to the roster of companies.

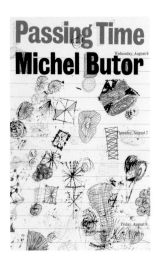

For a book jacket, the doodles, scribbles, and marks familiar to anyone who has sat passing time illustrate the title *Passing Time*.

While concepts such as academic freedom may seem intangible, they gain immediacy when interpreted through a nicely ambiguous visual metaphor. Here, lined-up pencils suggest both a barrier to the free speech of the title as well as symbols of it; but since two pencils are broken, the image also simultaneously suggests freedom and the loss of it. As Richard Saul Wurman said, "You only understand something relative to something you already understand."

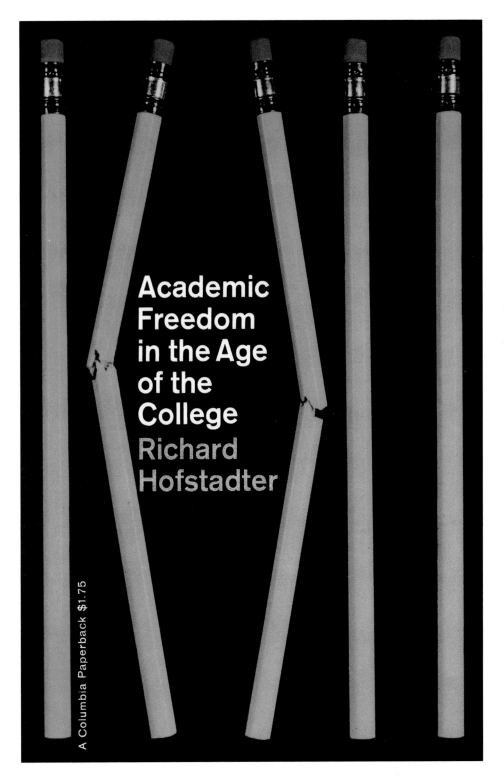

Moving air is easy . . . controlling it takes an expert

Moving air is easy . . . controlling it takes an expert

All the brawn in the world won't help this glass blower unless he has the ability to control it with the deft touch, the precise move that comes only with experience. Cooling and moving air can be tricky. We know because that's our business. Doing it efficiently, quietly and economically is our stock in trade. Over the years we have learned to control our production strength with creative design and imaginative engineering. You'll find the whole story in Brochure 102. Get a copy now from the Torrington Manufacturing Company, Torrington, Connecticut.

TORRINGTON

A mixture of nitrogen, oxygen, argon, carbon dioxide, helium, krypton, neon and xenon can be controlled in a musical instrument to bring enjoyment to millions. These same gases, commonly known as air, can also be piped through a high frequency whistle to summon an errant dog. In either case the air must be controlled to be effective. In our capacity as air moving specialists we have brought many complex problems to heel and won the applause of our customers. Write for Brochure 102 to the Torrington Manufacturing Company, Torrington, Conn.

TORRINGTON

Moving air is easy... controlling it takes an expert

The imperative blast of the Shofar has made the pages of Hebrew culture tremble for timeless centuries. Fashioned from the horn of a ram, this simple instrument has a range of only two basic notes separated by an interval of a fifth. Yet at the close of special ceremonies such as Rosh Hashana, the Shofar player can execute a powerful glissando which is prolonged until his breath gives out.
The wonders worked by experts spring many times from simple materials molded together with imaginative skill. The air moving equipment Torrington makes is a happy example of the state of this art.
The Torrington Manufacturing Company, Torrington, Connecticut.

Moving air is easy... controlling it takes an expert

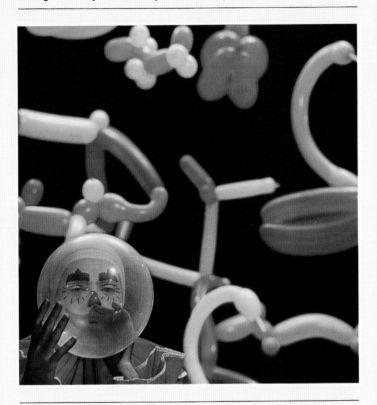

Who remembers the old time balloonman? A huff and a puff, a pinch and a tuck and you were staring wide eyed at a swan or an elephant or perhaps a purple clown. The art of the balloonman is nearly lost now, and his creations have faded into fantasy.
In our business of specialty blowers, we have designed some fantastic shapes, too, but with a purpose. Our craftsmen still know where to pinch and tuck to get the most out of a design. Happily our art is not being lost. It is stronger than ever before.
Write for brochure 102 to the Torrington Manufacturing Company, Torrington, Conn.

What could possibly be more ephemeral than thin air? Yet, in a series of trade advertisements, arresting images give the subject substance and force. Glass blowing, playing a wind instrument, the call to prayer through a ram's horn, and inflating playful balloons express the company's tag line: "Moving air is easy, controlling it takes an expert."

The actual air-moving equipment of the Torrington Manufacturing Company is shown too, but at a small size. It is the metaphorical images that sustain the reader's interest.

Sometimes, imagery can reinforce words, names, or meaning. Parachute, a Knoll furniture product, is visualized through parachute-related imagery. Only the well-known name of the company makes the connection to furniture.

The Van Cliburn Foundation logo is linked to the famous pianist by the elongated typeface that fancifully suggests a piano keyboard and music.

VANCLIBURNFOUNDATION

Knoll Parachute

GRILLER QUARTET

In a quartet, four individual musicians play as one. A single music stand super-imposed four times toys with that notion of unity and individuality, turning the stand into a music tree that symbolizes the four members of the Griller Quartet.

Time Inc. and Warner Communications each created products that were both seen *and* heard. This commonality sparked the idea of combining an eye and an ear into a single symbol for the merged Time Warner company, and later for Time Warner Cable.

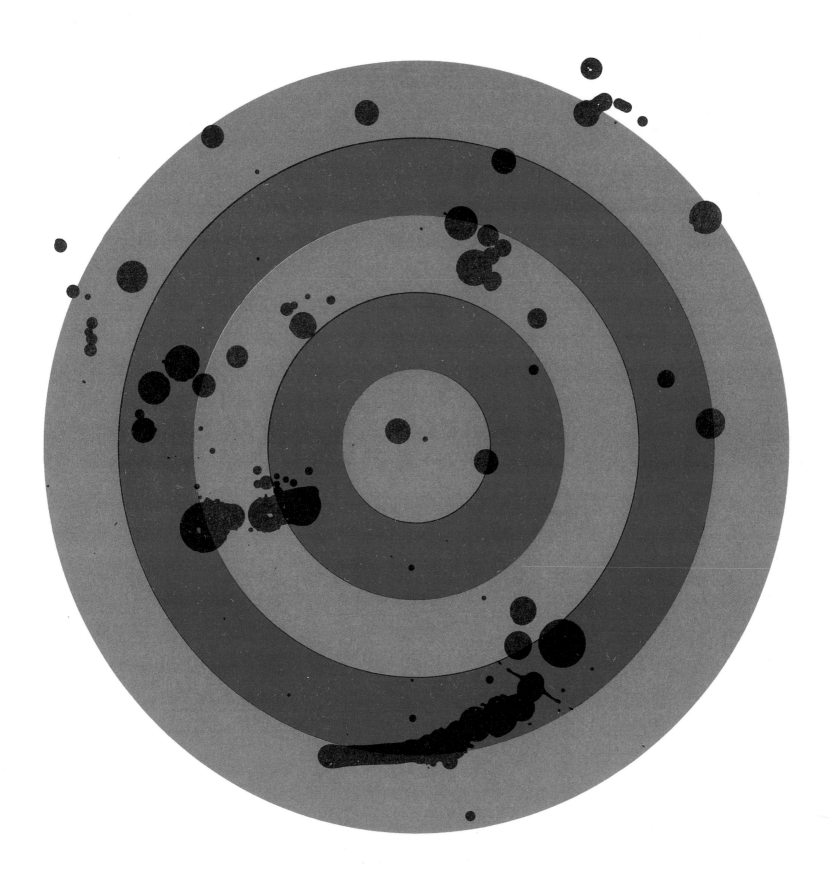

Artists and designers often use the materials of art and design to comment on art and design.

For a design magazine cover, spattering ink on a target instead of bullet holes or arrows symbolizes the complexity of graphic design, where few pieces successfully hit the bull's-eye.

On the cover of an issue of the *Journal of The American Institute of Graphic Arts*, scribbling and scratching serve as a symbol of graphic arts.

The notion of America as a melting pot ladles up a food analogy to describe the country's lively ethnic mix. For "A Nation of Nations," the 1976 bicentennial exhibition at the Smithsonian Institution in Washington, D.C., a collection of actual neon signs embraces the analogy, succinctly conveying the idea of the smorgasbord that is America. The variety of different countries represented is topped off by America's uniquely hybrid cuisines, represented by establishments such as Goldberg's Pizzeria or the Italian-French-Spanish Bakery.

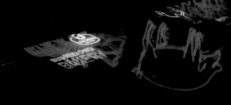

Commenting
Giving a voice to points of view

When cartoonist Thomas Nast began hectoring Tammany Hall in the 1870s, Boss Tweed supposedly demanded: "Stop them damned pictures. I don't care what the papers write about me. My constituents can't read. But, damn it, they can see pictures."

Images and graphics—whether in editorial cartoons, national symbols, political ads, or advocacy posters—are mighty tools for expressing beliefs, swaying opinion, and demonstrating commitment. They speak to us on a more visceral level than text. They can impart conviction and emotion in a way that words alone may not be able to do.

By using commonly understood imagery in provocative ways, the designer can express heartfelt feelings while avoiding the obvious—raising important issues while sidestepping the clichés that so often obscure or trivialize.

FOR THE LOVE OF LIFE
SUPPORT AIDS RESEARCH

Flowers are a symbol of life, of beauty, of growth. A lifeless, wilted flower, among the healthy ones demands our attention. It forces the question, "Why?"

Appropriating the familiar form and colors of a stop sign —right down to the usual small inscription at the bottom —gets across the "Stop AIDS" message without actually saying it. The enjoinder is all the more powerful because it comes from a deeply ingrained graphic symbol rather than from a line of text.

Emergence of Identity	Expressions of Identity	Crisis in Values	Future of Learning	Creativity and the Learning Process
The Right to Read	Myths of Education	Educational Hardware	Keeping Children Healthy	Making Children Healthy
Handicapped	Injured	Changing Families	Children and Parents	Family Planning Family Economics

Communicating the Law

Day Care

Children Without Prejudice

For a White House Conference on Children, simple flower drawings become metaphors for children and adults. This design forms the basis for a visual language in which the child-size and parent-size flowers were animated to express the wide variety of issues that were the subjects of conference reports.

To capture a childlike visual character, all the illustrations were drawn left-handed by the right-handed designer.

The Child Advocate

Environment

Child Development and Mass Media

Rights of Children

Leisure Time

Child Service Institutions

Humanity has many faces, and many ways to show them. The idea that despite apparent differences we are all one people is communicated on this poster through the faces of folk sculptures from various world cultures.

Suffragettes march together for equal rights at the polls in a 1975 poster for the television program "Shoulder to Shoulder." The drawing—a sea of resolute faces beneath no-nonsense hats—is meant to suggest a powerful wave, with those in front leading the unstoppable force of those coming up from behind.

PEACE 平和

Design: Seff Geissbuhler   Printing: Collton Graphic Co., Inc.

It's almost always easier to visualize a negative than a positive; to show what you're against rather than what you're for. Demonstrating against war is a frequent theme, expressed in every conceivable form. Pleading for peace is more difficult, and more rare.

Three peace posters commemorate the 40th anniversary of the bombing of Hiroshima.

One poster from the cold war era shows two giant beasts, Godzilla and King Kong, ambling hand in hand toward the future.

The raised, open palm of a young person amplifies the international gesture of peace, a gesture meant to halt conflict. At the same time, the intricate lines and creases of the enlarged hand suggest the uniqueness and sanctity of each individual life.

The classic, idyllic, peaceful image on an antique plate has been shattered, then crudely taped back together again. It speaks of the fragility of the plate—and of our world—and how difficult it is to put things right after they have gone wrong.

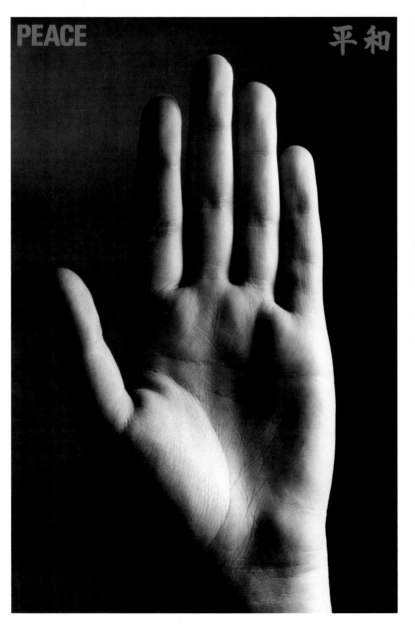

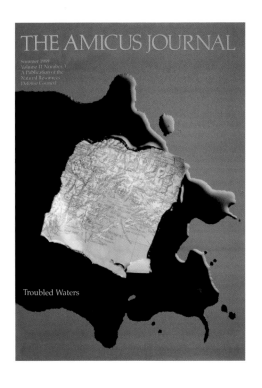

THE AMICUS JOURNAL

Summer 1989
Volume 11 Number 3
A Publication of the
Natural Resources
Defense Council

Troubled Waters

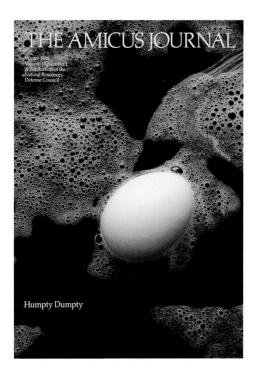

THE AMICUS JOURNAL

Winter 1988
Volume 10 Number 1
A Publication of the
Natural Resources
Defense Council

Humpty Dumpty

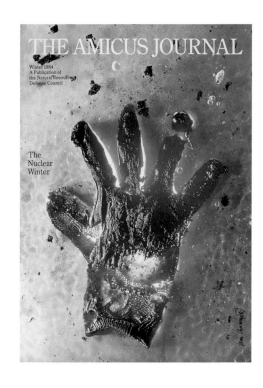

THE AMICUS JOURNAL

Winter 1984
A Publication of
the Natural Resources
Defense Council

The
Nuclear
Winter

THE AMICUS JOURNAL

Winter 1990
Volume 12 Number 1
A Publication of the
Natural Resources
Defense Council

The Population Explosion

THE AMICUS JOURNAL

Global Tomorrow
Today's New
Foreign Policy Crisis

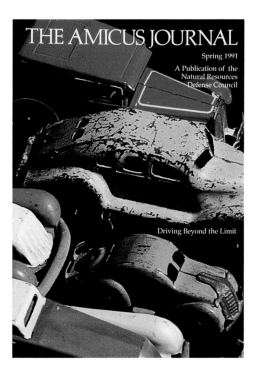

THE AMICUS JOURNAL

Spring 1991
A Publication of the
Natural Resources
Defense Council

Driving Beyond the Limit

THE AMICUS JOURNAL

Winter 1987
Volume 9 Number 1
A Publication of the
Natural Resources
Defense Council

California's
Vanishing
Wetlands

The cover of a magazine, book, or report presents a canvas on which to home in on a topic with a single, evocative image. Each issue of *The Amicus Journal,* a publication of the Natural Resources Defense Council, highlights a lead article that addresses a major environmental concern.

In "Troubled Waters," a map fragment of Prudhoe Bay, Alaska, torn out and floating in a pool of crude oil, recalls the disastrous oil spill in a fragile habitat.

"Humpty Dumpty" has had his fall... into polluted water, calling attention to a major problem everywhere. Even all the king's horses and men can't solve this dilemma.

"The Nuclear Winter" shows a hand, representing all of us, in a winter glove...frozen into a block of ice.

"Population Explosion" expresses the concept with the portrait of a person exploded into a multiple image.

"Global Tomorrow" depicts an inflatable globe collapsed when the air is taken out.

For "Driving Beyond the Limit," an old car spews filth beyond the limits of acceptability.

In "California's Vanishing Wetlands" a strip of tape holds down a feather. The resulting "X" implies that the marsh in the photograph is doomed.

TOWARD A SANE NUCLEAR POLICY

Graphic comments often exploit visual connections in order to say what words can't.

For a published essay on the issue of nuclear proliferation and its risks to the world as we know it, overlapping letters come ever closer together, finally arriving at a cohesive agreement on the word "policy."

The cover of an early edition of Bertrand Russell's *Common Sense and Nuclear Warfare* is built on the designer's observation that an atomic blast and a human brain share a common graphic form— a discovery at once arresting and disturbing.

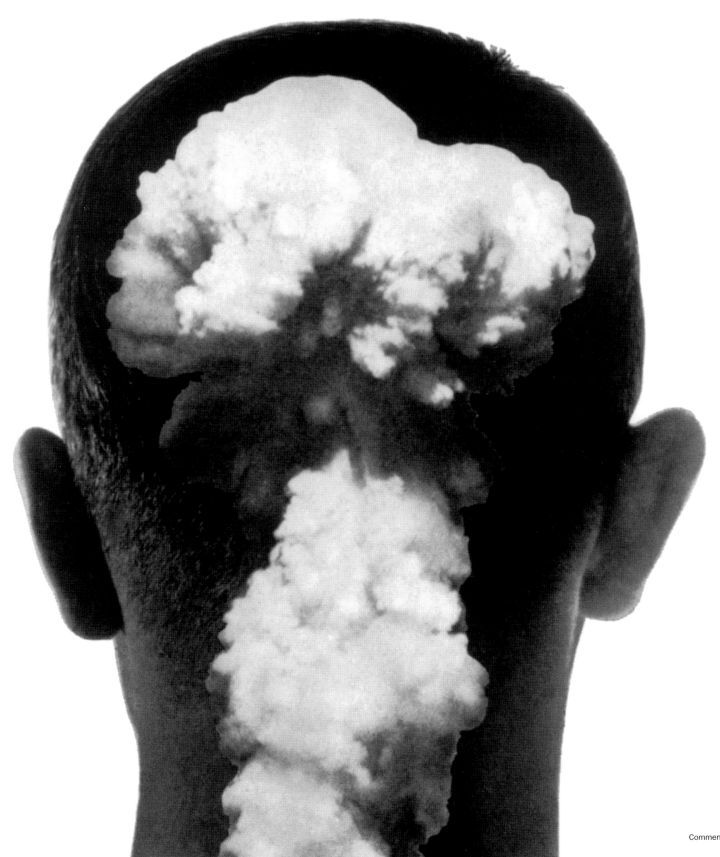

Images provoke emotions. Emotions can fire our imagination. Imagination makes us think.

The unexploded bomb (UXB) caught in a brick wall relates to a television drama about the dangerous task of defusing stray bombs in World War II England. The image is covered with a raw splatter of ink to express the risk of violence and mayhem.

The image of a gun split in two by a violent act renders the gun itself incapable of further violence. This 1958 image pre-dated the gun-control movement.

Earth is, of course, a spinning globe. But we are used to seeing it represented graphically as a flat surface, with north on top and south at the bottom. Flipping it "upside down" creates a disconcerting image that makes us rethink our precon-ceptions, as in this graphic developed for the United Nations Development Programme.

THE WORLD

a different perspective

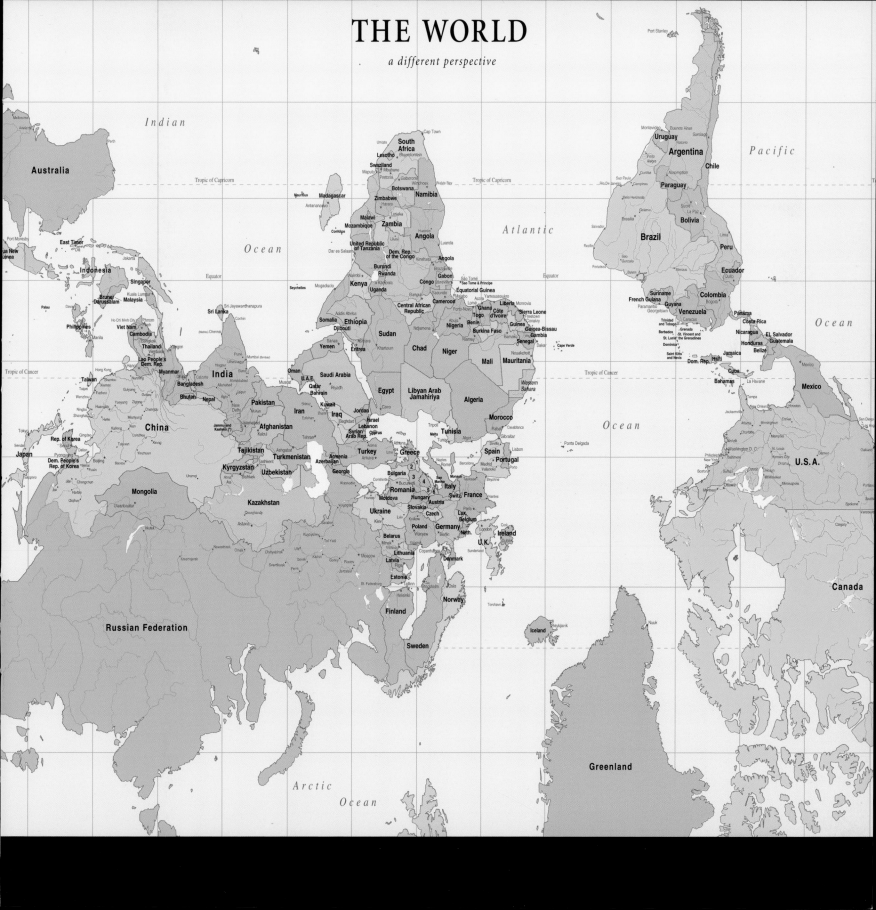

Indian

Australia

Ocean

Melbourne
Adelaide
Perth

Port Moresby
Papua New Guinea
East Timor
Dili

Indonesia

Jakarta

Singapor

Kuala Lumpur
Malaysia
Brunei Darussalam

Palau

Philippines

Manila

Viet Nam
Ho Chi Minh City
Cambodia
Bangkok
Phnom Penh
Thailand
Vientiane
Lao People's Dem. Rep.

Hong Kong

Myanmar
Yangon

Taiwan
Taipei

China

Rep. of Korea
Seoul
Dem. People's Rep. of Korea
Pyongyang

Japan
Tokyo
Sapporo
Sendai

Mongolia
Ulaanbaatar

Kazakhstan
Astana
Almaty

Beijing
Shanghai

Russian Federation

Sri Lanka
Sri Jayawardhanapura
Cochin

India
New Delhi
Mumbai (Bombay)
Pune
Chennai (Madras)

Bangladesh
Bhutan
Nepal

Pakistan
Karachi

Afghanistan
Kabul

Iran
Tehran

Tajikistan
Dushanbe
Turkmenistan
Ashgabat
Kyrgyzstan
Bishkek
Uzbekistan
Tashkent
Azerbaijan
Armenia
Georgia

Oman
Muscat
U.A.E.
Qatar
Bahrain
Saudi Arabia
Riyadh
Kuwait
Iraq
Baghdad
Jordan
Israel
Lebanon
Syrian Arab Rep.
Cyprus

Turkey
Ankara

Greece
Athens

Egypt
Cairo

Libyan Arab Jamahiriya
Tripoli

Algeria
Algiers

Tunisia
Tunis

Morocco
Rabat
Casablanca

Spain
Madrid
Barcelona

Portugal
Lisbon

Bulgaria
Sofia
Romania
Bucharest
Moldova
Hungary
Austria
Slovakia
Czech
Ukraine
Kiev
Belarus
Minsk
Poland
Warsaw
Germany
Berlin
Neth.
Belgium
Lux.
France
Paris
Switz.
Italy
Rome
Naples
San Marino
Monaco

U.K.
London
Ireland
Dublin

Lithuania
Vilnius
Latvia
Riga
Estonia
Tallinn

Denmark
Copenhagen

Norway
Oslo

Sweden
Stockholm

Finland
Helsinki

Iceland
Reykjavik

Greenland

Nuuk

Tropic of Cancer

Tropic of Cancer

Equator

Equator

Tropic of Capricorn

Tropic of Capricorn

South Africa
Cape Town
Bloemfontein
Lesotho
Swaziland
Maputo
Pretoria
Mbabane
Johannesburg
Gaborone
Windhoek

Botswana
Namibia
Walvis Bay

Madagascar
Antananarivo

Mauritius

Zimbabwe
Harare

Malawi
Zambia
Lusaka
Angola
Luanda

Mozambique
Comoros

United Republic of Tanzania
Dar es Salaam

Burundi
Rwanda
Dem. Rep. of the Congo
Kinshasa
Brazzaville
Congo
Gabon
Angola

Kenya
Nairobi
Uganda
Kampala

Seychelles

Somalia
Ethiopia
Djibouti
Addis Ababa

Sanaa
Yemen

Eritrea

Sudan
Khartoum

Chad

Ndjamena

Niger
Niamey

Mali

Mauritania
Nouakchott

Western Sahara

Central African Republic
Bangui

Cameroon
Yaounde

Equatorial Guinea
Malabo
São Tomé & Principe
São Tomé
Libreville

Nigeria
Abuja

Benin
Togo
Ghana
Accra
Porto-Novo
Lomé
Côte d'Ivoire
Yamoussoukro
Liberia
Monrovia

Sierra Leone
Freetown
Guinea
Conakry
Burkina Faso
Ouagadougou
Guinea-Bissau
Bissau
Gambia
Senegal
Dakar
Banjul

Cape Verde

Atlantic

Ocean

Ponta Delgada

Uruguay
Montevideo
Buenos Aires
Rosario
Argentina
Santiago
Chile
Asuncion
Paraguay
Porto Alegre
Curitiba
Rio De Janeiro
São Paulo

Brazil
Brasilia
Belo Horizonte
Goiania
Salvador
Recife
Fortaleza
Belem
Manaus

La Paz
Sucre
Bolivia

Lima
Peru

Quito
Ecuador

Bogotá
Colombia
Guyana
Georgetown
French Guiana
Suriname
Paramaribo
Cayenne
Venezuela
Caracas

Panama
Costa Rica
Nicaragua
Honduras
El Salvador
Guatemala
Belize

Trinidad and Tobago
Grenada
Barbados
St. Vincent and the Grenadines
St. Lucia
Dominica

Saint Kitts and Nevis

Jamaica
Haiti
Dom. Rep.
Cuba
La Havane
Bahamas

Mexico
Mexico
Guadalajara
Monterrey
Tampa

U.S.A.
Washington D.C.
New York
Boston
Philadelphia
Baltimore
Buffalo
Detroit
Chicago
Atlanta
Memphis
St. Louis
Kansas City
Dallas
Houston
New Orleans
Jacksonville
Miami
Minneapolis
San Antonio
El Paso
Phoenix
Denver
Salt Lake City
Los Angeles
San Diego
San Francisco
Oakland
Sacramento
Portland
Seattle
Spokane

Canada
Ottawa
Toronto
Montreal
Quebec
Calgary
Vancouver

Port Stanley

Pacific

Ocean

Ocean

Arctic Ocean

1
2
3
4
5
6

Telling stories
Making history come alive

Ask schoolkids about history. They often dismiss it as a dull roster of names and dates. Those same children, however, may eagerly embrace a storybook. But what is history if not a version of "once upon a time"? The word "story" is embedded in "history" for good reason.

Designers create visual stories that use images and environments to engage the audience. They can transform lessons into experiences, harnessing sight, sound, and space to help people feel a story and make connections.

Permanent exhibits at the Johnstown Flood Museum provide a dramatic account of the disastrous 1889 flood. More than 3,000 people perished in that calamity as the flood waters brought down a massive wall of debris that included telephone poles, railroad cars, and sections of buildings.

To convey a sense of the experience, and to dramatize the impact of the event, an imposing 60-foot-long, three-dimensional assemblage dominates the gallery space. In front of this massive image sits a small bottle of actual floodwater saved by a survivor.

Steerage-class immigrants to America arrived with all their worldly possessions in tow. In the Baggage Room, the entry to the Ellis Island Museum of Immigration, a large tableau of well-worn trunks, carpetbags, and suit-cases brings to life and humanizes the range of pos-sessions that each immigrant chose to bring to America.

A closer look at the artifacts prompts visitors to pause and think about the baggage —emotional and physical— that each person carried.

The photographs on the wall reflect the postwar exodus to the suburbs.

A CULTURE OF CONSUMPTION

The U.S. emerged from World War II as the world's economic powerhouse. America at mid-century had 7...

WOMEN'S POSTWAR WORLD

During the war, many women had taken good-paying jobs previously held by men. But peacetime brought an end to these opportunities...

Unlike written or spoken stories, a museum narrative includes movement. History exhibitions, for instance, often tell tales as a journey through a physical space that parallels the journey through time.

At the Harry S. Truman Presidential Library in Independence, Missouri, visitors pass a series of displays that evoke different periods and events from Truman's time in office. The idea: to provide a look at the context in which Truman's actions were taken.

As a prelude to its examination of the Marshall Plan and NATO, the installation portrays the postwar years of the late 1940s and early 1950s. In the United States, this era marked the beginning of the greatest economic boom in the nation's history. Millions entered the middle class, and countless families packed up and headed for the suburbs in pursuit of the American dream.

At the same time, much of Europe remained devastated by war and roiled by considerable political unrest. The next section of the exhibition, shown above, delves into this turmoil with monitors in a dark, rubble-strewn space, revealing what was happening across the Atlantic.

How can a designer draw a museum visitor into the story? One way is to physically immerse the audience in the narrative, surrounding them with an atmosphere or scene so that each visitor becomes a participant.

At the Truman Presidential Library, an enveloping section of an outside-in globe focuses on Asia. Through a combination of documentary video, narration, and lighting, this immersive environment tells the dramatic story of how the cold war became much hotter in the late 1940s and early 1950s as China turned Red, the Korean war exploded, and the first sparks of conflict in Vietnam crackled across the Pacific.

A different kind of immersion embraces visitors at the observation floor of the John Hancock building in Boston. Here, a darkened theater space features a scale model of the city. Sound, light, and projection effects dramatically depict Boston's physical growth and its role in the Revolutionary War.

When spinning a story, give the big picture. And give the small picture.

The broad view provides context and orients visitors. Small vignettes, however, nurture empathy and understanding. They add the human dimension, and a more manageable scale.

At the National D-Day Museum in New Orleans, a large wall display near the entrance to a series of galleries on World War II in the Pacific summarizes, in four minutes, the entire history of the Allied invasions. Sequential lighting effects, narration, sound, and an overhead LED message band combine to give a dramatic overview of the displays that follow.

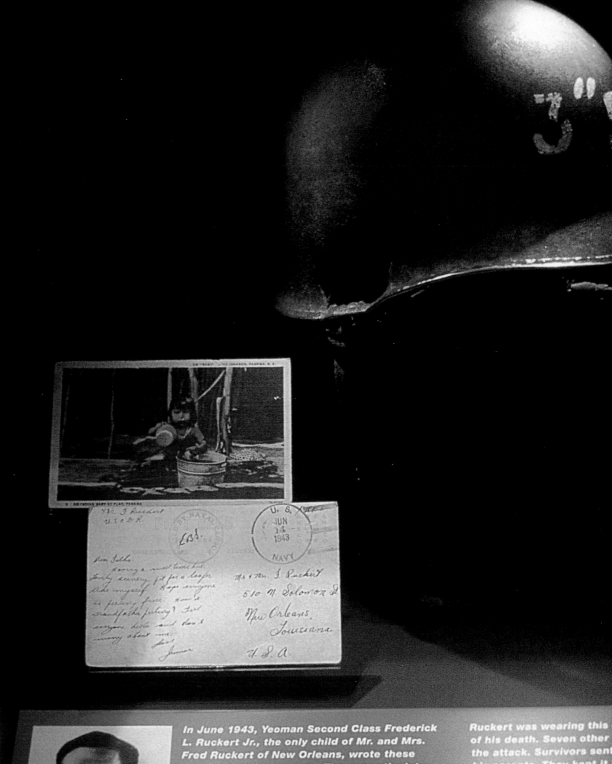

The meaning and impact of the larger D-Day story is conveyed through the personal and specific stories and voices of individuals involved in the war. These combine actual artifacts with accounts of incidents —told, where possible, in the individual's own words.

A POW's secret diary, kept hidden in an old coffee can with a false bottom, provides a very human story that tells more about the experience and the era than cold data and facts ever could.

The helmet with a large hole in it belonged to a Coast Guardsman killed on Guadalcanal. His fellow guardsmen sent the helmet to his parents. It is displayed along with letters he wrote.

In June 1943, Yeoman Second Class Frederick L. Ruckert Jr., the only child of Mr. and Mrs. Fred Ruckert of New Orleans, wrote these postcards to his parents. Three months later, Ruckert, a Coast Guardsman aboard LST 167, was killed near the island of Vella Lavella when Japanese aircraft dropped two bombs on his ship. **One bomb** penetrated the main deck and blew **through** the side of the ship. The other also went **through** the main deck and exploded on the tank deck, igniting 1,000 gallons of gasoline and 250 drums of oil.

Ruckert was wearing this ⬚ of his death. Seven other ⬚ the attack. Survivors sent ⬚ his parents. They kept it ⬚ keepsake of their lost so⬚ decades later. The marki⬚ helmet indicates Rucker⬚ 3-inch, 50-caliber main ⬚

In an exhibition, it's not just *what* you show but *how* you show it. That may seem self-evident, but even the obvious often bears repeating. Dramatic installation techniques infuse dry, factual stories with palpable interest and energy.

At the National D-Day Museum's introduction to World War II, a display vividly conveys the imbalance of power, in the late 1930s among the soon-to-be adversaries. National flags, scaled to the size of their armed forces, represent the military might of Japan, Germany, and the United States.

The flags are covered with small military figures, each representing 2,000 soldiers.

The Money Museum at the Federal Reserve Bank in Atlanta, houses a collection tracing the history of money, from barter to paper exchange. Alcove exhibits tell what the Federal Reserve does, explain the different forms money takes today, and reveal how counterfeit bills are discovered. One display features a globe made of credit cards.

Telling certain stories requires ingenuity to make the incomprehensible understandable and the theoretical visible.

The Library of Congress in Washington, D.C., houses the Sigmund Freud archives, which include many original manuscripts. The manuscripts are displayed in alcoves organized by theory. Video clips of Freudian references in popular culture—made by Sean Connery, Homer Simpson, Woody Allen, and others—anchor the end of each alcove.

Visitors leaving the exhibit confront a curving wall with stacked images from contemporary magazines, book covers, and web pages. These document the pervasive impact of Freud's influence on our culture.

In planning a major exhibit of Freud's papers, it quickly became clear that almost no one would be able to read them since they are in Old German, and almost illegibly written in an archaic penmanship style. The idea of using "exploded manuscripts" helped make the documents more understandable. Below each manuscript page is a photo reproduction of the page with an important passage highlighted. A yellow plaque provides an English translation of that passage; other, smaller plaques offer commentary on its significance from different viewpoints. A photo shows Freud at the time he wrote each document.

c. 1937

construction

Freud used the word "construction" to mean an extensive interpretation that aims to reconstruct a portion of a person's past, usually a person's childhood.

We do not pretend that an individual construction is anything more than a conjecture which awaits examination, confirmation or rejection. We claim no authority for it, we require no direct agreement from the patient, nor do we argue with him if at first he denies it.

What makes an analyst's interpretation true? What makes it effective? On what basis should it be confirmed or rejected? The issue of how to judge analytic interpretations has remained controversial, from Freud's time to our own.

Constructions in Analysis

Throughout his career Freud often considered what it was that made an analytic interpretation effective and how it might be proven true. How were the interventions of the analyst different from the suggestions of a hypnotist? In this essay from late in his life, Freud returned

The Third Avenue "El" was very fast but very loud.

Edgar Allan Poe "haunted" this neighborhood.

780 Third used to serve great burgers.

Now that was a lot of trains.

A little imagination transforms a temporary construction bridge (required to protect pedestrians during maintenance on a high-rise office building) into a neighborhood gift (*not* required, but hugely appreciated). To celebrate the history of Turtle Bay, a display of paintings, maps, and historic photos depicts the story of this Manhattan neighborhood. An actual history exhibit—despite its unorthodox format and location—the display even included an extensive bibliography.

An exhibition for a major public corridor at the New York Public Library honors the past and present of this famous cultural institution. By combining artifacts, rare books, personal accounts, recordings, and historic film with large-scale photography, the installation recounts the history of the library, highlights its treasures, and introduces the diverse programs and services it offers.

A booklet tells the story of making 100% cotton paper and the role that recycling plays in it. The booklet's cover is made of the unbleached cotton from which the paper springs. Photographs depict each step in the manufacturing process, while text on facing pages describes what's going on. The type is arranged to suggest the action being shown and described. Material, photography, and typography work as one to convey a technical story in an interesting and informative way.

PRISMA

Remember the boy who cried "wolf"? When the big, bad wolf finally showed up, no one heeded the lad's warning. His message was vital, but its effect had been neutered by overuse. Designers regularly confront that same danger. In a world filled with visual clutter, images and words constantly compete for our attention. Design can explore new approaches that avoid tired clichés, or can revive well-established symbols by placing them in a surprising context that provokes a second look... and a second thought.

Ideally, a cliché-busting approach should grow logically—if unexpectedly —from the subject at hand. Like an Agatha Christie mystery, the design solution should be unforeseen, yet, once known, seem almost self-evident, the inevitable conclusion.

GREY

The logo for a children's discovery center in San Juan, Puerto Rico, might have featured each letter in a different color. Instead, the letters have been joined and then overlaid with bands of color that disregard where the letters themselves begin or end. In this manner the color transitions are more gradual, less rigid, and the overall effect is more unusual... and prismatic.

The obvious color for Grey Advertising is gray. But the best way to make the global agency stand out is to avoid the obvious. So Grey becomes red.

For a lithographer, the instinctive image to choose would normally be something colorful, something lovely, something that shows off the techniques of color printing. This trade advertisement takes the opposite tack, spotlighting instead a clean-up press rag shown in black-and-white. The unexpected image attracted considerable attention and demanded closer examination.

This rag cleaned the presses that printed the finest Annual Reports, Brochures, Displays, Posters, and Magazine Insert Pages for America's most discriminating Printing Buyers. In the hands of our Craftsmen it helped us serve the American Thread Company; Curtiss Wright Corporation; De Laval Separator Company; National Lead Company; Pan American World Airways; Pepsi-Cola Company; Singer Sewing Machine Company, and others. **Colorcraft Lithographers,** Inc./175 Varick Street/New York 14, N. Y./CHelsea 3-2100

Entitled "Footnose," the collage for an artist's exhibition expresses the ability of art to be contrary, to make new connections, to observe forms, color, and context and hence make discoveries that are not obvious. A footprint in the center of a face becomes a nose. The counter in the letter P can then be a mouth. A fragment of the letter O is a cap, or hair. Even the toes, because of their position, take on the qualities of a moustache.

A portrait usually highlights its subject. This illustration for a poster obscures its subject, hiding Winston Churchill behind a haze of smoke. Yet, though certainly not the obvious solution, it makes sense. When combined with the television show's title *Winston Churchill: The Wilderness Years*, it is clear that, even without his visage visible, the homburg and cigar connote Britain's prime minister, and do so in an original way.

The New York
Philharmonic

Phone Festival
Philharmonic Week
February 23 - 26, 1978
Presented with WQXR

Marbles and musical notes.
That's not a combination
that comes to mind naturally.
But somehow, the marbles
do fit on the musical staff.
The pairing works, and the spots
of color in the glass seem
musical in this context. The
rough, spaced out hand lettering
captures the same spirit of
invention and composition.

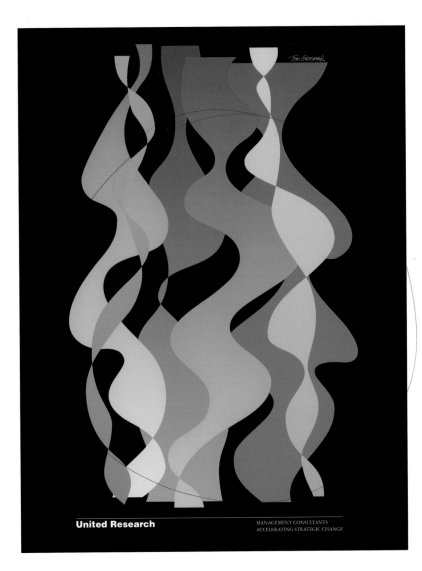

Two dance program advertisements convey the feeling of ballet, using shape, color, and movement without resorting to literal imagery.

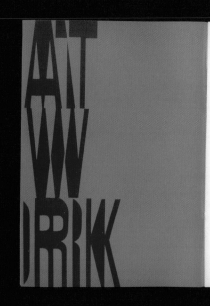

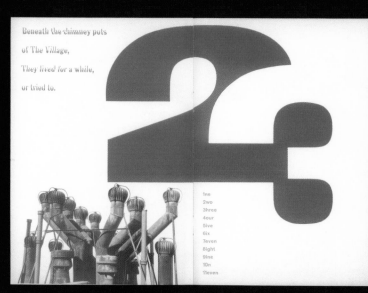

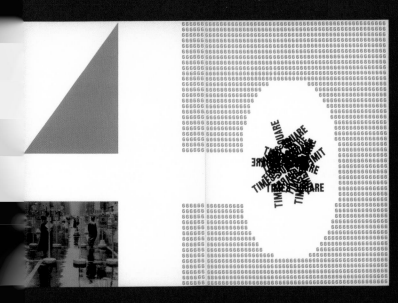

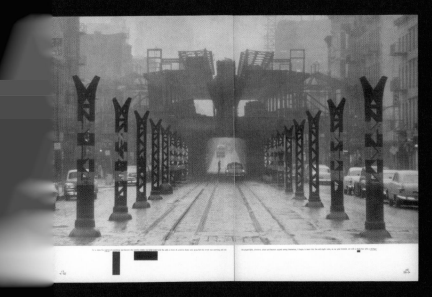

In the pages of an experimental typography booklet, published in the late 1950s, type is used as a medium for its own sake, purposely disregarding conventional expectations.

There was a time when I would detour to avoid walking anywhere on **Seven**th Avenue south of 40th to 34th. I ne**ver liked Eighth**

Avenue, either, **and still** don't. I have developed an affection for M**acy's no**w that The Great Department Store i**s giving way to T**

he Shopping Center. Wanamaker's was at its best during the years w**hich car**ried it gradually downhill to its end. I **do not understa**

nd those who failed to not**ice this long descent and had to be surpri**sed w**hen the end came. They are children **who are used**

to being protected against** the facts of the slaughterhouse. What g**reat per**ception is needed to know that a de**partment store**,

office building or theatre is like a tree or shrub? Yet, many do not k**now thi**s. I can understand the young not kn**owing because,**

to them, a tree seems to h**ave existed and promises to exist forev**er. But t**he middle-aged and the old? I am bo**red, too, with th**

e conceit that depicts hero**ic edifices such as the Brooklyn Bridge o**r the Wo**olworth Building as challenging nat**ure. They are na**

ture. In art, though, as in th**e forest, certain forms are destined for **longer lif**e than others. Fortunately, man has **permitted conti**

nuing life to the violin, the **J**ensen letter and the bicycle, despite th**e fact th**at the points of their full developme**nt have long sin**

ce been reached. Not so with New York. New York cuts down both **its trees** and its buildings, not only long befo**re they have die**

d, but long before they hav**e been able to demonstrate their ability **to live. I**n the beginning of the love affair wit**h New York, ign**

orance of the ways of the b**eloved is bliss. At this stage, it's simply t**he view** of her face that matters. You ask no q**uestions of the**

purplish airbrush tones be**yond the lower Manhattan skyline, seen **from th**e deck of the bridge's first gothic tow**er: no docume**

ntation is required for yell**ow skyscraper lights or wooden-car rattle **of Bro**oklyn-bound el trains. Later, with its **necessities, com**

es knowledge of the doing**s of newspaper barons, political bosses, p**rosecu**ting attorneys, architects and city plan**ners, reformer**

s, peddlers, pickpockets and** public relations men. In the end, thoug**h, you** go back to the bridge at twilight, ba**ck to the bridge.**

Sociology has recorded the view that the real estate business—a floating crapgame in which is invested

legislative, judicial and executive powers—is in the background of New York's contemporary history of

grandfathers vanishing into old people's homes and young wives putting off having babies for another

year. A horseplayer might end up his day at Belmont with winnings enough for hamburgers and a pad

in a Times Square hotel for the night; or, he might lose and have to borrow a fin from another horse-

player to get him out to the track the next day. But a real estate gambler's day might bring about a

traffic jam that could endanger the health and welfare of millions, lead to the narrowing of miles of

sidewalk and cause the Air Pollution Control Commission to petition the Board of Estimate for an in-

crease in its annual appropriation. Who ever heard of a testimonial dinner being given to a horseplayer?

Spuyten Duyvil Sheepshead Bay Tavern-on-the-Green Yeshiva John Wanamaker McSorley's Old Ale House Park Row MacDougal Alley Lüchows Knickerbock er Longacre Square Abraham Cahan Floradora Wallabout Market Frannces Tavern Carl Van Vechten Jacob Schiff Horace Mann Van Cortlandt Onderdonck Lefferts Hippodrome Mercer Street Rhinelander Patchin Place Ozone Park Eugene O'Neill Murray Hill Paddy's Market Corlears Hook Gravesend Minett a Lane Great Kill Muhlenberg Horn & Hardart Florenz Ziegfeld Kingsbridge Alfred E. Smith Hudson Dusters Rivington Street Clason Point Washington Irving Pineapple Street Guggenheim Sandy Hook Flatiron Henry Ward Beecher Broadway Yorkville Williamsburg Vanderbilt Maiden Lane Tiffany's Har ry K. Thaw Triborough Natnan Straus Strunsky's Love Stables Washington Square Alfred Stieglitz Boris Thomashevsky Sands Street John A. Roebling Fla tbush Fieldston Jacob Riis Joseph Pulitzer Pitkin Avenue Isaac M. Singer Moshulu Parkway Gouverneur Morris J. Pierpont Morgan George Gershwin Petipas F. W. Woolworth Morningside Heights Reginald Marsh Harlem R. H. Macy & Co. Otto H. Kahn High Bridge Harrigan and Hart Fort Tryon Robert Goelet Desbrosses Street Hell Gate Gansevoort Jay Gould Fort Clinton Flushing Coogan's Bluff Greeley Herald Square Gowanus Fort Totten Dyckman Stuyvesant Dutch Kills Delancey Coney Island Cherry Lane Chatham Square Trinity Yard Cavanagh's Bowery Canarsie Delmonico Bryant Chelsea Greenpoint Fulton Bushwick Brooklyn Bronx de Peyster Carnegie Triborough Arthur Kill Bellevue Algonquin Abingdon Cooper Beekman Amsterdam Far Rockaway Altman Ebbets Field Aspinwall Brevoort Bowling Green Cartier's Fort Greene Sailors Snug Harbor Astor Brownsville Belmont Bleecker Biltmore Spuyten Duyvil Sheepshead Bay Tavern-on-the-Green Yeshiva John Wanamaker McSorley's Old Ale House Park Row MacDougal Alley Lüchows Knickerbocker Longacre Square Abraham Cahan Floradora Wallabout Market Frannces Tavern Carl Van Vechten Jacob Schiff Horace Mann Van Cortlandt Onderdonck Lefferts Hip podrome Mercer Street Rhinelander Patchin Place Ozone Park Eugene O'Neill Murray Hill Paddy's Market Corlears Hook Gravesend Minetta Lane Great Kill Muhlenberg Horn & Hardart Florenz Ziegfeld Kingsbridge Alfred E. Smith Hudson Dusters Rivington Street Clason Point Washington Irving Pine apple Street Guggenheim Sandy Hook Flatiron Henry Ward Beecher Broadway Yorkville Williamsburg Vanderbilt Maiden Lane Tiffany's Harry K. Thaw Triborough Natnan Straus Strunsky's Love Stables Washington Square Alfred Stieglitz Boris Thomashevsky Sands Street John A. Roebling Flatbush Field ston Jacob Riis Joseph Pulitzer Pitkin Avenue Isaac M. Singer Moshulu Parkway Gouverneur Morris J. Pierpont Morgan George Gershwin Petipas F. W. Woolworth Morningside Heights Reginald Marsh Harlem R. H. Macy & Co. Otto H. Kahn High Bridge Harrigan and Hart Fort Tryon Robert Goelet Des brosses Street Hell Gate Gansevoort Jay Gould Fort Clinton Flushing Coogan's Bluff Greeley Herald Square Gowanus Fort Totten Dyckman Stuyvesant Dut ch Kills Delancey Coney Island Cherry Lane Chatham Square Trinity Yard Cavanagh's Bowery Canarsie Delmonico Bryant Chelsea Greenpoint Fulton Bushwick Brooklyn Bronx de Peyster Carnegie Triborough Arthur Kill Bellevue Algonquin Abingdon Cooper Beekman Amsterdam Far Rockaway Altman Ebbets Field Aspinwall Brevoort Bowling Green Cartier's Fort Greene Sailors Snug Harbor Astor Brownsville Belmont Bleecker Biltmore Spuyten Duyvil Sheepshead Bay Tavern-on-the-Green Yeshiva John Wanamaker McSorley's Old Ale House Park Row MacDougal Alley Lüchows Knickerbocker Longacre Square Abraham Cahan Floradora Wallabout Market Frannces Tavern Carl Van Vechten Jacob Schiff Horace Mann Van Cortlandt Onderdonck Lefferts Hip podrome Mercer Street Rhinelander Patchin Place Ozone Park Eugene O'Neill Murray Hill Paddy's Market Corlears Hook Gravesend Minetta Lane Great Kill Muhlenberg Horn & Hardart Florenz Ziegfeld Kingsbridge Alfred E. Smith Hudson Dusters Rivington Street Clason Point Washington Irving Pine apple Street Guggenheim Sandy Hook Flatiron Henry Ward Beecher Broadway Yorkville Williamsburg Vanderbilt Maiden Lane Tiffany's Harry K. Thaw Triborough Natnan Straus Strunsky's Love Stables Washington Square Alfred Stieglitz Boris Thomashevsky Sands Street John A. Roebling Flatbush Field ston Jacob Riis Joseph Pulitzer Pitkin Avenue Isaac M. Singer Moshulu Parkway Gouverneur Morris J. Pierpont Morgan George Gershwin Petipas F. W. Woolworth Morningside Heights Reginald Marsh Harlem R. H. Macy & Co. Otto H. Kahn High Bridge Harrigan and Hart Fort Tryon Robert Goelet Des brosses Street Hell Gate Gansevoort Jay Gould Fort Clinton Flushing Coogan's Bluff Greeley Herald Square Gowanus Fort Totten Dyckman Stuyvesant Dut ch Kills Delancey Coney Island Cherry Lane Chatham Square Trinity Yard Cavanagh's Bowery Canarsie Delmonico Bryant Chelsea Greenpoint Fulton Bu shwick Brooklyn Bronx de Peyster Carnegie Triborough Arthur Kill Bellevue Algonquin Abingdon Cooper Beekman Amsterdam Far Rockaway Altman Ebbets Field Aspinwall Brevoort Bowling Green Cartier's Fort Greene Sailors Snug Harbor Astor Brownsville Belmont Bleecker Biltmore Spuyten Duyvil Sheepshead Bay Tavern-on-the-Green Yeshiva John Wanamaker McSorley's Old Ale House Park Row MacDougal Alley Lüchows Knickerbocker Longacre Square Abraham Cahan Floradora Wallabout Market Frannces Tavern Carl Van Vechten Jacob Schiff Horace Mann Van Cortlandt Onderdonck Lefferts Hip podrome Mercer Street Rhinelander Patchin Place Ozone Park Eugene O'Neill Murray Hill Paddy's Market Corlears Hook Gravesend Minetta Lane Great Kill Muhlenberg Horn & Hardart Florenz Ziegfeld Kingsbridge Alfred E. Smith Hudson Dusters Rivington Street Clason Point Washington Irving Pine apple Street Guggenheim Sandy Hook Flatiron Henry Ward Beecher Broadway Yorkville Williamsburg Vanderbilt Maiden Lane Tiffany's Harry K. Thaw Triborough Nathan Straus Strunsky's Love Stables Washington Square Alfred Stieglitz Boris Thomashevsky Sands Street John A. Roebling Flatbush Field ston Jacob Riis Joseph Pulitzer Pitkin Avenue Isaac M. Singer Moshulu Parkway Gouverneur Morris J. Pierpont Morgan George Gershwin Petipas F. W. Woolworth Morningside Heights Reginald Marsh Harlem R. H. Macy & Co. Otto H. Kahn High Bridge Harrigan and Hart Fort Tryon Robert Goelet Des brosses Street Hell Gate Gansevoort Jay Gould Fort Clinton Flushing Coogan's Bluff Greeley Herald Square Gowanus Fort Totten Dyckman Stuyvesant Dutch Kills Delancey Coney Island Cherry Lane Chatham Square Trinity Yard Cavanagh's Bowery Canarsie Delmonico Bryant Chelsea Greenpoint Fulton Bushwick Brooklyn Bronx de Peyster Carnegie Triborough Arthur Kill Bellevue Algonquin Abingdon Cooper Beekman Amsterdam Far Rockaway Altman Ebbets Field Aspinwall Brevoort Bowling Green Cartier's Fort Greene Sailors Snug Harbor Astor Brownsville Belmont Bleecker Biltmore Spuyten Duyvil Sheepshead Bay Tavern-on-the-Green Yeshiva John Wanamaker McSorley's Old Ale House Park Row MacDougal Alley Lüchows Knickerbocker Longacre Square Abraham Cahan Floradora Wallabout Market Frannces Tavern Carl Van Vechten Jacob Schiff Horace Mann Van Cortlandt Onderdonck Lefferts Hip podrome Mercer Street Rhinelander Patchin Place Ozone Park Eugene O'Neill Murray Hill Paddy's Market Corlears Hook Gravesend Minetta Lane Great Kill Muhlenberg Horn & Hardart Florenz Ziegfeld Kingsbridge Alfred E. Smith Hudson Dusters Rivington Street Clason Point Washington Irving Pine apple Street Guggenheim Sandy Hook Flatiron Henry Ward Beecher Broadway Yorkville Williamsburg Vanderbilt Maiden Lane Tiffany's Harry K. Thaw Triborough Nathan Straus Strunsky's Love Stables Washington Square Alfred Stieglitz Boris Thomashevsky Sands Street John A. Roebling Flatbush Field ston Jacob Riis Joseph Pulitzer Pitkin Avenue Isaac M. Singer Moshulu Parkway Gouverneur Morris J. Pierpont Morgan George Gershwin Petipas F. W. Woolworth Morningside Heights Reginald Marsh Harlem R. H. Macy & Co. Otto H. Kahn High Bridge Harrigan and Hart Fort Tryon Robert Goelet Des brosses Street Hell Gate Gansevoort Jay Gould Fort Clinton Flushing Coogan's Bluff Greeley Herald Square Gowanus Fort Totten Dyckman Stuyvesant Du tch Kills Delancey Coney Island Cherry Lane Chatham Square Trinity Yard Cavanagh's Bowery Canarsie Delmonico Bryant Chelsea Greenpoint Fulton Bushwick Brooklyn Bronx de Peyster Carnegie Triborough Arthur Kill Bellevue Algonquin Abingdon Cooper Beekman Amsterdam Far Rockaway Altman Ebbets Field Aspinwall Brevoort Bowling Green Cartier's Fort Greene Sailors Snug Harbor Astor Brownsville Belmont Bleecker Biltmore Spuyten Duyvil Sheepshead Bay Tavern-on-the-Green Yeshiva John Wanamaker McSorley's Old Ale House Park Row MacDougal Alley Lüchows Knickerbocker Longacre Square Abraham Cahan Floradora Wallabout Market Frannces Tavern Carl Van Vechten Jacob Schiff Horace Mann Van Cortlandt Onderdonck Lefferts Hip podrome Mercer Street Rhinelander Patchin Place Ozone Park Eugene O'Neill Murray Hill Paddy's Market Corlears Hook Gravesend Minetta Lane Great Kill Muhlenberg Horn & Hardart Florenz Ziegfeld Kingsbridge Alfred E. Smith Hudson Dusters Rivington Street Clason Point Washington Irving Pine

As soon as a designer ignores the expected and looks at the inherent characteristics of a subject, the possibility of finding new formats arises.

Crane Papers produced a booklet to address common misconceptions among designers about the limits of the engraving process. To overcome the old stigmas, and to emphasize the tactile quality inherent in engraving, the design employs contemporary images of a sort not usually associated with engraving, including paint spatters, brushstrokes, and images bleeding off the page.

Annual reports all present similar information, and invariably fit a standard format. But when something is invariable, that's the time to vary it. Even when the company makes musical instruments, there's nothing obvious about turning the report into a memorable keepsake by putting it on a long-playing record.

Commercial real estate brochures usually feature conventional building photographs. But who says they must? Collaged fragments of building photographs, leases, and maps convey thematic points, asserting a bold attitude in a series of brochures for Insignia ESG.

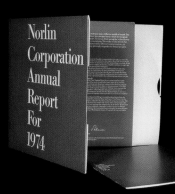

Norlin Corporation Annual Report For 1974

The benefits of unmatched experience

The same ESG resources used by New York City's largest business and professional firms are available to all of our clients. Whatever the size of your organization, it can draw on ESG's full team of experts. Our experience with the most challenging transactions is applied to meeting your firm's needs.

ESG has served law and accounting firms, advertising agencies, entertainment companies, publishing houses, garment companies, nonprofit groups, financial service companies, and banks and insurance companies, to name just a few. Whether their space is measured in tens or hundreds of thousands of square feet, our commitment to them, and to the highest level of professional conduct, remains the same.

Sony Corporation of America's transaction with AT&T for the entire building on Madison Avenue was distinguished by the intricate problems of converting a custom-designed 710,000 sq. ft, 35-story landmark. To accommodate its New York headquarters, Sony needed a large space that could foster a creative environment and support state-of-the-art computers and telecommunications. ESG undertook a massive effort to see if the building designed especially for AT&T could be adapted to Sony's operations. The sheer size of the transaction — over half a billion dollars — carried significant financial and accounting implications for these two publicly-held companies. There were other difficult issues as well, such as transferring building management to Sony, and transforming the ground floor area into the Sony Plaza retail space. ESG helped reconcile the complex operating, financial, and accounting objectives of AT&T and Sony to forge an historic transaction in which the requirements of both sides were satisfied.

Investment Sales and Financing

ESG is proficient in all financial aspects of real estate: investment sales, financing, sale leaseback, and securitization.

For owners of real estate, we offer customized sales programs that are scheduled to be completed in six to nine months. ESG has earned a stellar reputation for marketing commercial real estate due to our extensive market knowledge, close corporate relationships, and detailed database of potential buyers. We are equally adept at representing buyers of commercial property. ESG has the ability to identify and evaluate buildings for potential acquisition, assessing the need for capital improvements, and providing a clear picture of likely cash returns.

We also have the capability of matching property owners with capital sources to finance acquisitions or to refinance existing portfolios. ESG's excellent relationships with many leading financial institutions and pension funds give us leverage to negotiate the best possible terms for borrowers.

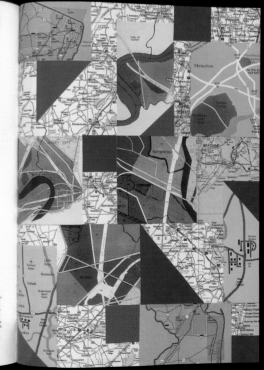

When NYNEX **Properties Company** was looking for real estate investments in northern Bergen County, it chose ESG to help with the search. ESG first helped NYNEX establish a price range and other investment criteria, then used our listing system to identify properties that might be for sale. The building ESG recommended was a three-story, 123,000 sq. ft. shell at 123 Tice Boulevard, in Woodcliff Lake - a prime location in the area with New Jersey's greatest concentration of corporate headquarters. Because it was NYNEX's first speculative investment, with no existing cash flow, the company was particularly interested in ESG's expertise and knowledge of the rental market. Within a relatively short period of time the entire building was leased to Sony Corporation of America, making it one of NYNEX's most successful real estate investments.

Avoiding the expected sometimes means forgetting the conventional rules before you begin.

A yellow parallelogram—in a Litchfield, Connecticut, meadow—confounds the viewer. A rectangle is believable. A parallelogram is not. Because the structure is not believable, visitors sometimes walk out to touch the wall, thinking that the perspective is very strange. How could a rectangle look like that?

The artist Claes Oldenburg, of soft sculpture fame, has many original thoughts about art. He deserved a soft book, long and wide enough to bend, made with vinyl over foam instead of boards. The title is not so obvious either. It is drafted the way we usually speak, not the way we usually write.

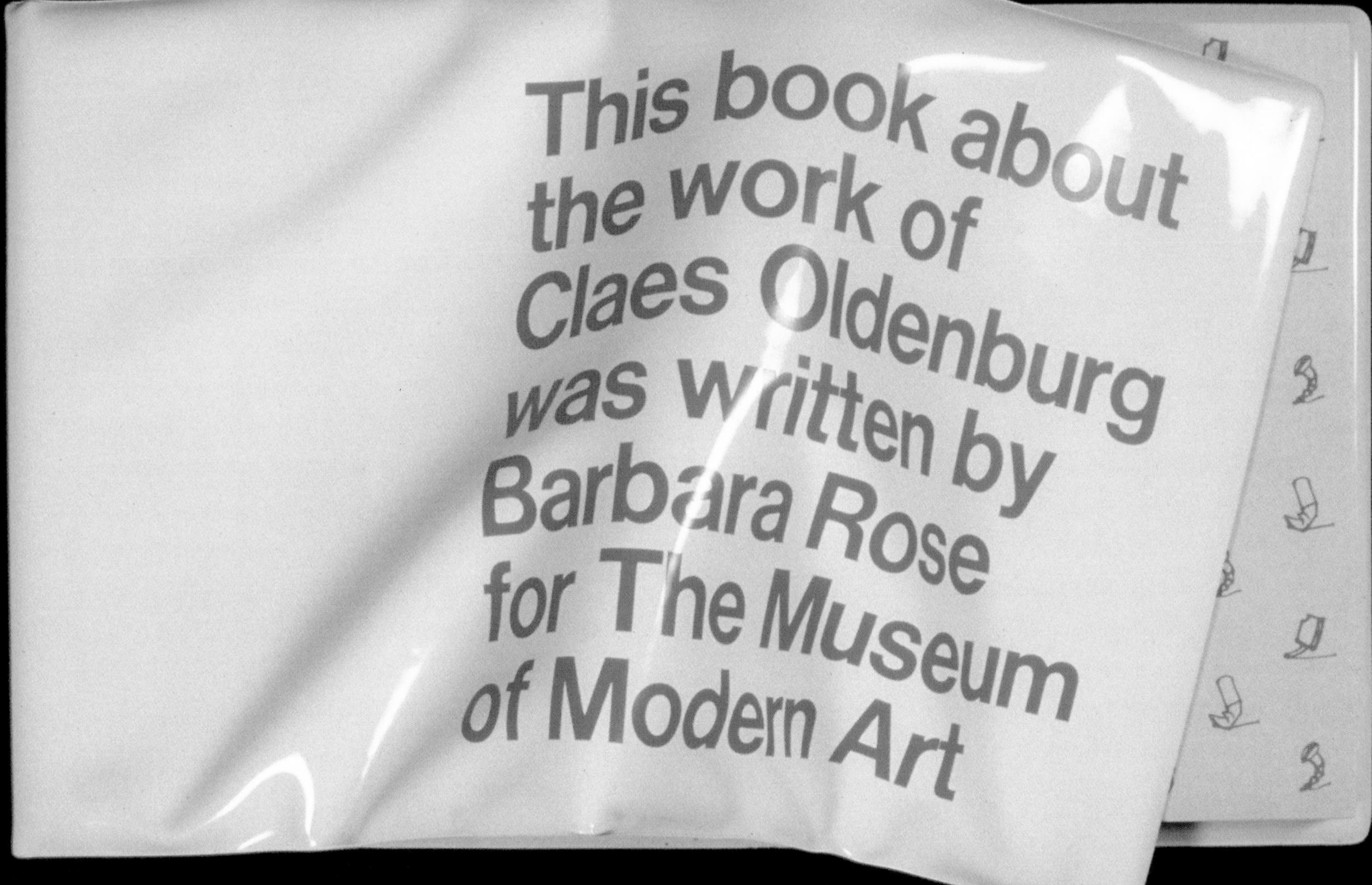

This book about
the work of
Claes Oldenburg
was written by
Barbara Rose
for The Museum
of Modern Art

In *The Hound of Baskervilles*, the dog's bark is famously significant because it is absent. Sometimes, the best way to call attention to a thing is to flamboyantly ignore it. An absence can be provocative.

A small section of a teaching exhibition on Yale University's large collection of furniture and decorative arts celebrated the modern architects and designers Charles and Ray Eames. The obvious approach would have been simply to present the Eames chairs. The not-so-obvious solution was to spotlight the inventive, structural bases of the chairs.

Herman Miller wanted to convey the attributes of its office systems in a series of magazine advertisements. Rather than feature the products, the design shows a world conspicuously empty of furniture. The message to the reader? Before you choose any office furniture you must understand the tasks that different workers perform. You must consider too that people come in different sizes, different sexes, and have different needs.

One ad highlights the various tasks different people perform. The other drives home a similar point in a different way by facetiously making all the workers identical.

The environment people work in should be designed around the work they do.

Imagine an office environment that takes its cues from the tasks people perform. That is infinitely adjustable, allowing swift, cost-effective response to changing needs.

Imagine, too, an advanced systems knowledge base, developed over years of research and refined in experience. An intelligence that ensures effective facility planning and management—before, during and after your move.

The Action Office® system by Herman Miller. It's more than a place to work. It's a way to work better.

Send for our booklet, A Sensible Approach to Facilities. Herman Miller Inc., Marketing Department, Zeeland, MI 49464.

herman miller

Sales education facilities in Atlanta, Boston, Chicago, Dallas, Detroit, Houston, Los Angeles, New York, San Francisco, Washington, D.C., Amsterdam, Basel (Herman Miller AG), Brussels, London, Paris, Toronto and other key cities internationally.

Should an office treat its inhabitants alike?

Imagine, instead, an environment that takes its cues from the differences between people. That is highly supportive to individual needs and personalities, infinitely adjustable, and responsive to changing work activities and communication patterns.

Imagine, too, an advanced systems knowledge base, developed over years of research and refined in experience. An intelligence that ensures effective facility planning and management—before, during and after your move.

The Action Office® system by Herman Miller. It's more than a place to work. It's a way to work better.

Send for our booklet, A Sensible Approach to Facilities. Herman Miller Inc., Marketing Department, Zeeland, MI 49464.

herman miller

Sales education facilities in Atlanta, Boston, Chicago, Dallas, Detroit, Houston, Los Angeles, New York, San Francisco, Washington, D.C., Amsterdam, Basel (Herman Miller AG), Brussels, London, Paris, Toronto and other key cities internationally

What is packaging for? Generally, it's just something to hold a product. But that's the usual answer, not the innovative one.

Poly Rods is a construction toy of sticks and connectors. The unusual packaging design puts the pieces inside the thick walls of the package, creating objects that are themselves toys—stackable to form an attractive display (and as much fun to play with at home as the Poly Rods).

To understand the problem of waste and garbage disposal, kids at the Children's Museum of Manhattan lift bags to feel the weight of trash from different societies. They learn that New Yorkers throw away almost twice the amount of waste as do residents of Tokyo.

Reinterpreting the familiar
Celebrating nature

Designers are always looking for new interpretations, using established visual symbols in new combinations to visualize complex ideas. The simpler and clearer the symbols, the more useful they become and the easier they are to combine with one another to achieve a new message.

UCLA summer sessions are geared to students who want to be achievers. One brochure cover uses colored pencils as symbols of art programs in design, film, and architecture. They are young shoots, ready to grow. On another cover, a paintbrush dipped in many colors casts the shadow of a palm tree, an image redolent of both Southern California and creativity, and thus appropriate for summer art and design studies in Los Angeles.

It all started with mammoths and bison and birds. These were the Bodoni and Helvetica of their time — the "fonts" with which the earliest cave artists recorded life. (In those days, typefaces really did have faces.) The earliest hieroglyphs were stylized versions of natural forms. Animals, rocks, rivers, and trees were not just subjects for sketches and landscapes, they were the forms and images through which people communicated. They still can be.

Borrowing from nature is among the most powerful and ancient techniques. Which is not surprising. Though she's never been honored by the AIGA or roasted at the Art Directors Club, Mother Nature is an unsurpassed designer.

The Master Series: Ivan Chermayeff

Expressive symbols are all around us in everyday objects. To discover them and reappropriate them is as much a part of the design process as creating something from scratch.

A glove can become a provocative stand-in for the hand. In this brochure cover, the colored pencil is a creative tool wielded by an unseen artist.

The double-ended red and blue pencil announces a course taught jointly by two people. The pencil is sharp and clean on one end, chewed and worn on the other, a symbol of two different personalities joined together in one classroom at the School of Visual Arts in New York.

A wooden pencil fashioned from a whole tree is frozen in mid-sketch on a brochure cover — a simple idea that sparks many associations. It's easy to imagine this pencil drawing yet another tree, which perhaps gives birth to another pencil...

A leafy twig as a pen, dipped into an ink bottle, combines the medium and the message for "An Essay on Nature."

Design is often inspired by nature, whose creativity and variety is unending. The intricacies and variations of fall leaves; the infinite array of forms, colors, textures, and patterns in a forest; the range of composition and surprise found in nature is unsurpassed. We can only marvel at it... and be inspired by it.

A hand-cut flower depicts the freshness of Shinsegae's product choices on packages, wrapping papers, delivery vehicles, and stores. The symbol was designed to appeal particularly to women, the vast majority of the customers of this South Korean department store chain.

Visit The New York Botanical Garden Conservatory. MTA gets you there.

Metropolitan
Transportation
Authority

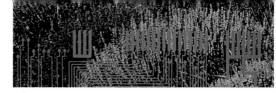

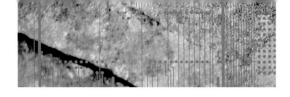

KLAUS SCHULZE PICTURE MUSIC

KLAUS SCHULZE MINDPHASER

KLAUS SCHULZE TRANCEFER

KLAUS SCHULZE DUNE

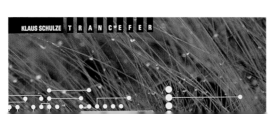

Juxtapositions bring out differences. They also reveal unexpected similarities and commonalities.

A series of recordings for Gramavision combines nature photographs (especially textural subjects) with modern musical notations, and technological symbols and circuits to express the complex layering of sounds found in new age music.

Flowers made from the crumpled sheet music of a piece by Mozart express the beauty of composition in this fundraising poster for the New York Philharmonic. The handwriting contributes to the immediacy and freshness of the annual campaign, adding a personal flair to an institutional message.

Say it again. But say it differently.

Reinterpreting similar subject matter is always a design challenge. How many times can you create an original and memorable symbol for an aquarium? After all, a fish is a fish is a fish, as Gertrude Stein might have said. Aquariums all over the world obviously have much in common with one another, yet there are specific differences.

An ambiguous image of both fish and waves for the National Aquarium in Baltimore reflects the institution's broad marine theme.

A combined shark and breaking wave represents the New Bedford (Massachusetts) Aquarium.

A single abstracted fish symbol from 1963 identifies the New England Aquarium in Boston.

In this mark for the Lisbon Aquarium in the Portuguese capital, the space between the creatures becomes a pattern that suggests light reflecting on the surface of water.

In the logo (opposite page) for the Tennessee Aquarium in Chattanooga, an array of shapes comes together to form an intricate puzzle of fish and fowl, divided by the course of the Tennessee River and its tributaries. The creatures' eyes turn into rising air bubbles.

www

Fire and water. These eternal elements of nature are opposites, negating each other. They are powerful forces, destructive at times and working together at others. Both can threaten humans, and both are vital to us. As symbols, fire and water provoke a host of complex associations.

When the publishers Harper & Row, with their logo of a torch, merged with Wm. Collins, with its fountain symbol, an opportunity was born. The resulting design joins the essence of both symbols, fire and water, into a new icon for the new company, HarperCollins.

The initial "W" in the symbol for Waterside is wavelike, when repeated, suggesting the East River location of the New York City residential housing development. Of course, this design came long before "www" connected us to the world via the web.

The Osaka Aquarium presents the marine life that thrives around the circle of volcanic Pacific islands and atolls known as the "Ring of Fire." The symbol draws a literal circle of red fire surrounding the blue water of the Pacific Ocean.

The sun is a universal symbol for life, light, youth, renewal, warmth, and growth. It has identified countless organizations and entities. Its ubiquity makes it a difficult symbol to employ in an original way.

The red "o" from the logo of Mobil Oil becomes a dawning sun in this poster for Young Audiences, an organization that sponsors theatrical events for children. The Young Audiences symbol itself was intentionally made in a child-like manner in the mid-1960s.

A rising sun is also the symbol for the Sunshine Cinema in New York City. It appears on the movie house's marquee.

The sun for Artear's channel 13, a major TV network in Buenos Aires, is made up of four 3-pointed crown shapes shifted and rotated into each other.

The Smithsonian Institution has used various versions of the sun as its emblem for decades. A consolidated approach merges all the incarnations into a single symbol that can be used consistently by the Smithsonian's 17 museums and myriad research centers around the world.

Stars, like suns, are a much-used symbol. They embody notions of excellence, achievement, and awards of all kinds, from military rank to hotel and restaurant ratings. Broadway and Hollywood have claimed the star as well to herald the most popular celebrities.

Stars shaped almost like dancing figures express the Christmas season at Saks Fifth Avenue. On each gift box and each store awning, a slightly different-shaped star danced in celebration of the holiday.

By moving around five equal-size star shapes, the negative space between them evolves into a capital "M" for Multicanal, the largest cable television network in Buenos Aires. The stars surrounding and shaping the "M" allude to a five-star rating.

The parent star/eagle, with its offspring, conveys the idea of protection for the American Republic Insurance Company.

For the American Film Institute, a five-pointed star moving through a 35mm frame suggests a film clip.

The American Bicentennial Theater poster suggests a chorus line of colorful stars and star-studded performances.

The Kennedy Center and Xerox Corporation present

American Bicentennial Theater

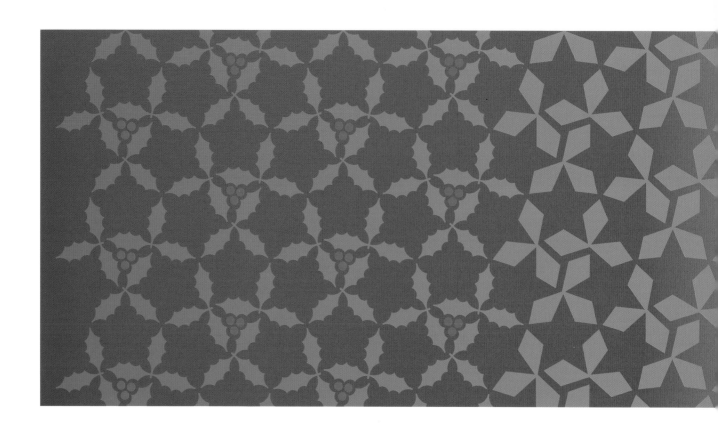

GEMINI

A play of positive and negative shapes and forms illustrates the idea of transformation and seasonal change on these Gemini Consulting holiday cards. Each transition culminates in a star form, a part of the firm's identity. The color gradations and use of dark and light colors enhances the perception of the figure-ground flux.

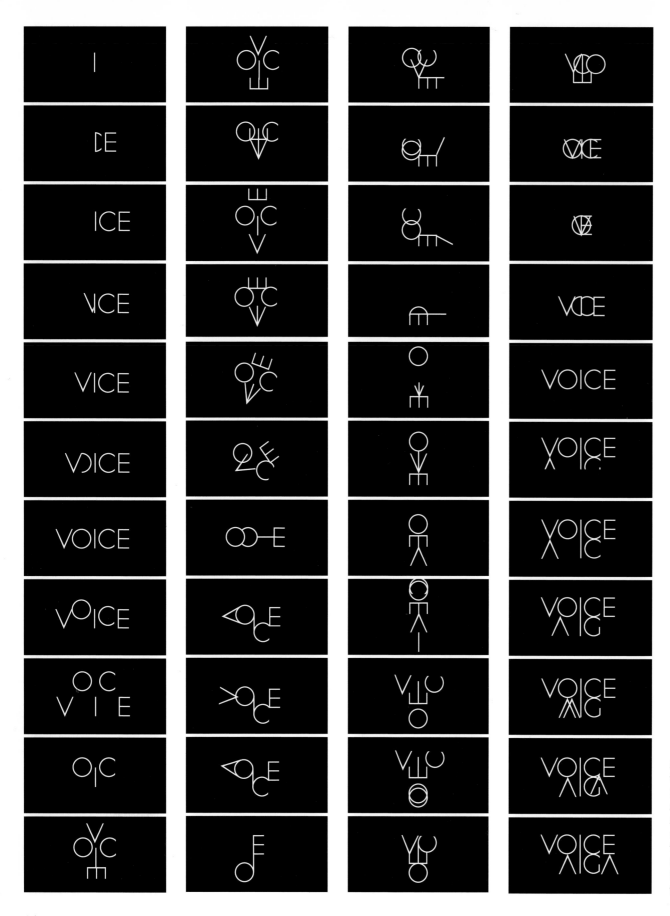

A 60-second animation captures the theme title "Voice" in a presentation at an American Institute of Graphic Arts conference. The animation used only the pure letterforms, and was accompanied by miscellaneous animal and human noises—the varied voices of nature.

Vertically arranged type becomes part of the landscape when integrated into a photograph of a city for a Neighborhood Conservation Conference poster. Shifting a negative and positive film transformed the photo into a striking image, a special effect of mysterious dimensionality. The literal photograph evolves into an abstract urban texture.

On a button for a the conference, the type itself becomes the landscape.

The simple house shape, a rectangle topped with a triangle, is a familiar symbol for home, family, shelter and all that they connote.

Linked symbols of houses, shown above, form an identity for Assisted Living Communities.

"CASA," which means "house" in both Spanish and Italian, is also the acronym for Center for Addiction and Substance Abuse. The double meaning creates a strong visual/verbal mark, with text and image very much at home together.

The Poets House logo, below, appears here at *twice* actual size.

The little red "tree house," a playhouse for young children, reinterprets the traditional house form in its own quirky way. Built with parts of real trees penetrating the walls and roof, it clearly is made for children, with windows and doors too small for parents to enter comfortably.

Demystifying data
Explaining abstract concepts

How do you convey the real meaning of a number? How much is one billion? You can use an analogy. For example, if we measured age in minutes rather than years, counting from the year 1 we would just recently have reached the one billion minute mark.

We also can express quantity visually. In developing plans for a major museum on the Holocaust, the design team learned that in a single day at Auschwitz-Birkenau, the Nazis murdered 20,000 people. How could the exhibition make visitors feel the enormity of that number? It was decided to gather 20,000 photographs of victims — photos taken by the Nazis — and to fill a large field of columns from floor to ceiling with them. There would be nothing else in the space. At the exit there would be a simple statement: "There are 20,000 portraits in this room. This is the number of people murdered at Auschwitz-Birkenau in a single day."

Schoolbooks used to teach that the brontosaurus had a brain the size of a pea. This was helpful because none of us had ever seen a brontosaurus, but all of us have encountered peas.

Eighty percent is just a number. "Four out of five doctors" is a much more evocative way of expressing the same amount.

In both these examples, data is infused with meaning and made more powerful by evoking concrete references.

Design can strive to do likewise. Presenting information clearly, smartly, or even eloquently is not always enough. To convey a message, designers may need to find inventive ways to dramatize the data's significance, communicating and explaining complex ideas simply, boldly, and memorably.

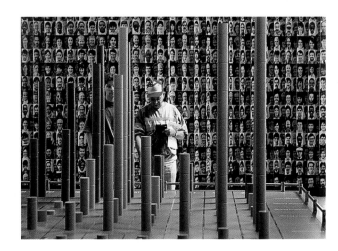

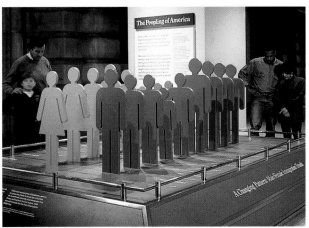

Statistics can be dry and dull. But they don't have to be. Direct audience interaction can make facts and figures dynamic, intriguing, and meaningful.

The Ellis Island Museum of Immigration in New York Harbor focuses on the short time at the end of the 19th century and the early 20th century when there was a great wave of migration to the U.S. One room, however, was set aside to convey, through statistics, the larger picture of U.S. and world migration patterns.

A vast globe brings the numbers to life, as moving, sequential lights show the density and flow of people around the globe over three centuries. Another display, this one of cutout figures, depicts how the ratio of men to women immigrants has changed over 250 years.

The photo at top shows a large walk-around bar chart. From one vantage point, it shows changes in the regions from which immigrants to the U.S. have come over the last two and a half centuries. From another viewpoint, the color-coded bars show how patterns of migration from each major region (e.g., Asia) have changed radically over the same time period. Thus, the visitor establishes a tangible relationship with the chart, gaining more information by physically interacting with it.

The language of chemistry is one of symbols and formulas. To much of the general public, it's utterly incomprehensible.

The American Chemical Society celebrated its 100th anniversary with a large traveling exhibit. The goal was to illustrate how chemistry has changed the quality of our lives—improving our health and affecting our lives in myriad ways. The exhibit was composed of seven large "pods," each devoted to a different aspect of the story. Each pod, in turn, featured symbolic display units that used elements of each theme arranged in ways that elucidate the subject.

A great variety of pills, capsules, and tablets, reflected by mirrors into infinity, symbolize the diversity of medicines today, all precisely designed for a very specific purpose.

Matter is in constant motion. The vigor of motion determines whether matter is gas, liquid, or solid. Balls in three compartments represent molecules in the different states.

Toy cars ranging from high performance race cars to multiple-axle trucks, are in motion to suggest that highly specialized machines are powered by highly specialized fuels.

Primary geometric forms, served up on dinner plates, remind us that all foods break down into six basic categories.

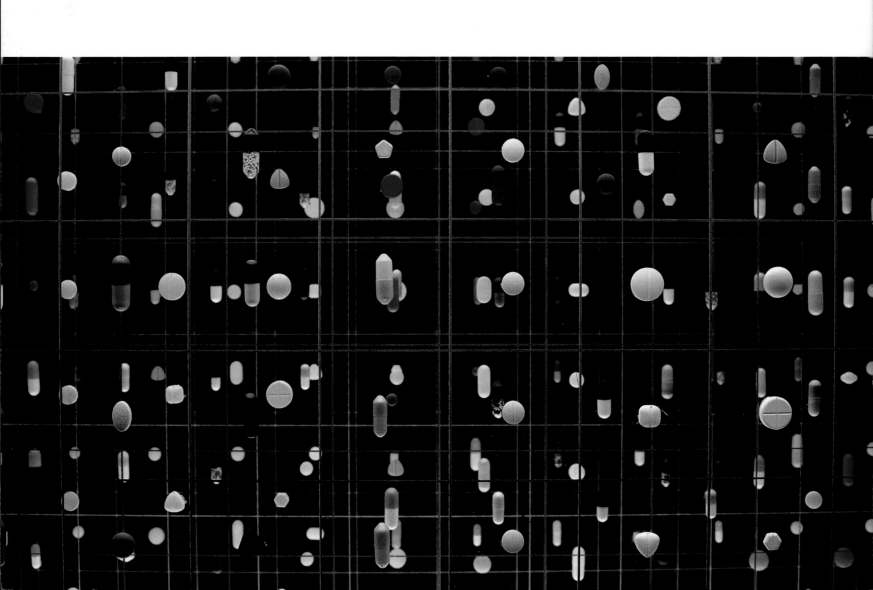

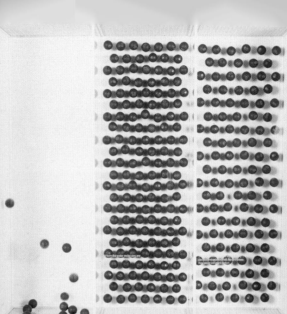

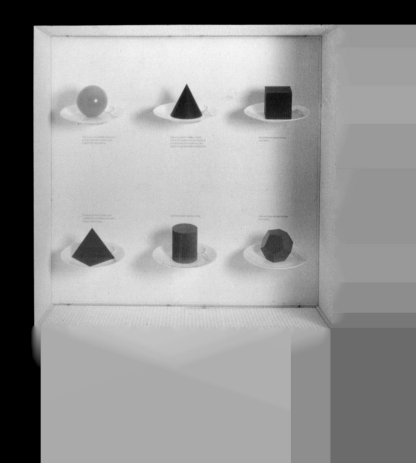

"Show and tell" is a classroom staple. And, as any schoolkid can testify, it's often the "show" part that does most of the telling. The lesson is that, at times, data can be conveyed more forcefully, and with more layers of meaning, when visual expression amplifies the verbal facts.

For instance, one can state that, out of 100 robin's eggs hatched, only 10% will live to adulthood. But words alone hardly carry the impact of that statistic. This display, a component of the World of Birds at the Bronx Zoo, relates the same information visually, dramatically, and sequentially.

Pictures of birds illustrate that if 100 robin's eggs turn into nestlings, only 74 will live. As the nestlings become fledglings, only 52 survive. A mere 10 fledglings from the original 100 eggs reach adulthood. As each creature is eliminated, a plaque appears in place of its picture, stating

the cause of its demise. The exhibition notes that the 90 that die before adulthood do live on in a way...feeding other creatures in the cycle of life.

Familiar images and metaphors can jog the memory or provide a frame of reference. They make complex events more understandable and more immediately meaningful.

At the John F. Kennedy Presidential Library, a graphic time line provides a context for documents and artifacts recounting major events of the Kennedy administration.

The time line relates these events to world affairs, scientific discoveries, and milestones in sports, entertainment, art, and literature. Sparking memories and associations, it anchors the narrative by evoking a specific time and place.

At the Smithsonian Institution, an exhibition entitled, "If We're So Good, Why Aren't We Better?" uses the metaphor of preparing an apple pie for a Thanksgiving dinner to explain the basic components of productivity. It shows the basic elements of any manufacturing process: a quintessential mom (labor); her stove, pots, and pans (tools); her ingredients (materials); and her recipes and her calculations for how much is needed (system). The next gallery shows what happens if her calculations are wrong. Here, a 10-foot-wide pie sits next to a two-inch one.

Herself (worker)   Appliances and utensils (tools)   Ingredients (materials)   A recipe (system)

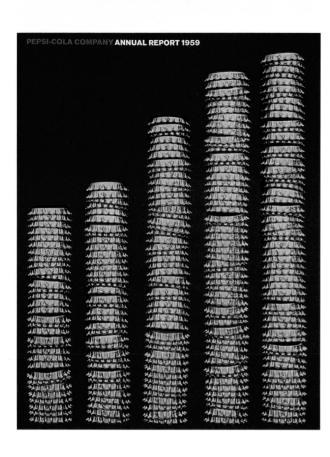

In annual reports, charts are essential, unavoidable... and usually pretty dull. But not necessarily. Sometimes, a judicious integration of images related to the institution issuing the report can make charts more attractive and accessible without lessening their credibility or obscuring their content.

For example, stacked bottle caps represent the five-year growth in sales of Pepsi-Cola products—a far more individualized and interesting annual report graph than the traditional bar chart.

To track financial data, charts from an annual report for the Hechinger Company, a lumber and hardware store chain for the do-it-yourself market, utilize products sold in the company's stores.

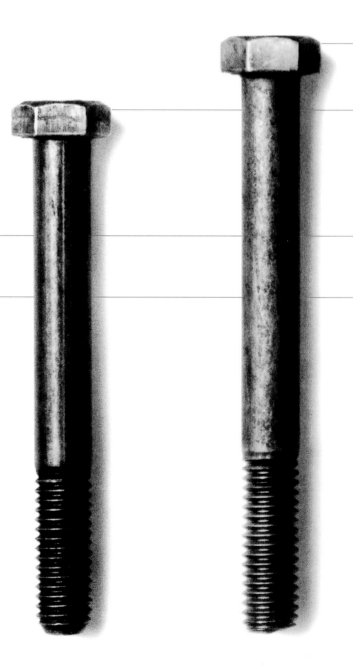

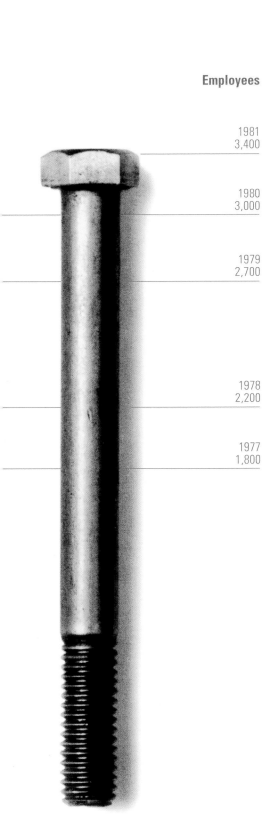

Employees

1981
3,400

1980
3,000

1979
2,700

1978
2,200

1977
1,800

1981
$210.6

1980
$170.4

1979
$146.8

1978
$111.2

1977
$92.6

Net Sales
(millions of dollars)

To make highly technical information interesting and attractive is always a challenge. The pieces shown on this spread were developed as promotions for paper companies and intended for use by designers.

The examples below are from a series of brochures explaining technical considerations that designers must bear in mind when preparing artwork for printing on uncoated papers. Imaginative photography demonstrates the various effects that are possible, uniting words and pictures. Each production technique is described technically in the adjacent text.

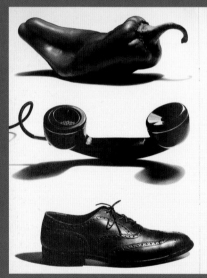

Dot Shape Patterns

Crane's Global Guide is a stationery design reference for international companies. With clear and precise graphics, it brings together unusual comparisons of measurement systems, weights, currency, telephone access codes, formats, and stationery standards to provide a useful reference tool.

Expressing personality
Crafting a visual identity

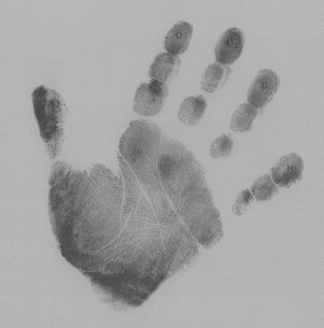

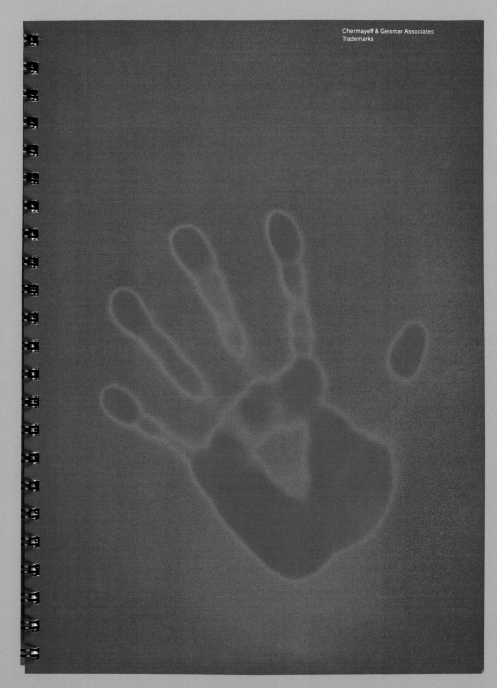

Chermayeff & Geismar Associates
Trademarks

A black smudge and domed derby evokes Chaplin. A jutting chin becomes FDR, or maybe Jay Leno; with a few, well-chosen flourishes, the caricaturist captures a character. Identity graphics must do the same. Shape and line, color and composition, typography and text also can bring a character to life— quickly, simply, memorably.

But design must create a persona without a person. It must highlight not a nose or chin or hat, but a less tangible corporate culture and mission. Stolid, familiar, spunky, elegant, intelligent— the rich vocabulary of adjectives we use to describe an individual finds its counterpart in an equally rich design vocabulary. The first challenge, then, is to recognize the essential nature of an entity. The second is to craft an appropriate visual language, a distinctive voice that speaks recognizably in any medium, from logo and letterhead to print and promotion.

A handprint, like the footprint of a newborn, is unique
to each individual. Yet, at the
same time, it is common
to us all. As such it can be an
effective graphic device,
simultaneously unique and
universal. On the facing page,
a handprint in blue ink conveys the idea of "Touch" for a
thematic exhibition. The
image not only works with the
concept, but also with the
title, thanks to the discovery
that the word "touch" has five
letters — one for each finger.

A catalog of trademarks
designed by Chermayeff &
Geismar features a cover
made of a material that holds
heat-sensitive liquid crystals
under a film. This makes
the simple act of touching the
book a design process of
sorts. Consciously or not,
readers leave their own temporary "trademark" on the
cover merely by touching its
surface.

For the Alvin Ailey dance
company, brushstroke figures
spell out the name of this
exuberant, jazz-oriented dance
group. The words themselves
prance and dance across the
page, with the central figure
combining the "v" of Alvin and
the "A" of Ailey.

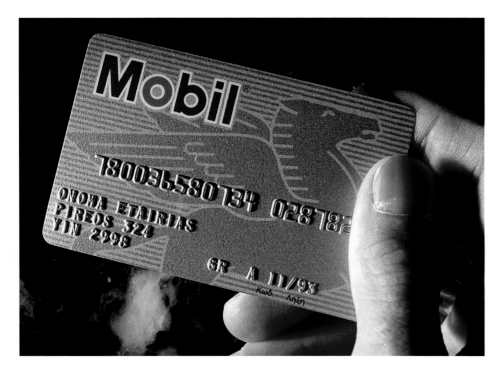

Unless you happen to be Dr. Jekyl, it's not hard for a person to maintain a coherent public profile. It can be more challenging, though, for a multifaceted corporation, an entity composed of many individuals and showing diverse faces through many activities. Thoughtful design can offer a solution, particularly if it has support at the highest levels of the organization.

In the 1950s and 1960s, Mobil Oil confronted a new identity issue. As Americans migrated to the suburbs in increasing numbers, oil companies such as Mobil found that they were being zoned out of the new communities because of their service stations' less than graceful appearance. Recognizing the problem and facing it head-on, Mobil undertook a comprehensive design program to make their facilities and products more attractive (and, with the later introduction of self-service, easier to use). A comprehensive design approach integrated new graphics with the new architecture. A fresh logo, which emphasized the "o" in the brand name, became a key component. So too did a specially

drawn alphabet that is used on everything from signs to credit cards, packaging, and even pump labels and instructions.

Mobil's traditional symbol, the flying red horse, did not fly away. A simplified Pegasus, placed on a white disk, adds color and personality to Mobil stations and products.

abcdefghijklm
nopqrstuvwxyz
ABCDEFGHIJKL
MNOPQRSTVW
XYZ1234567890
$¢£¥‰&?!←1 1
Mobil←%ŒÆØÇ

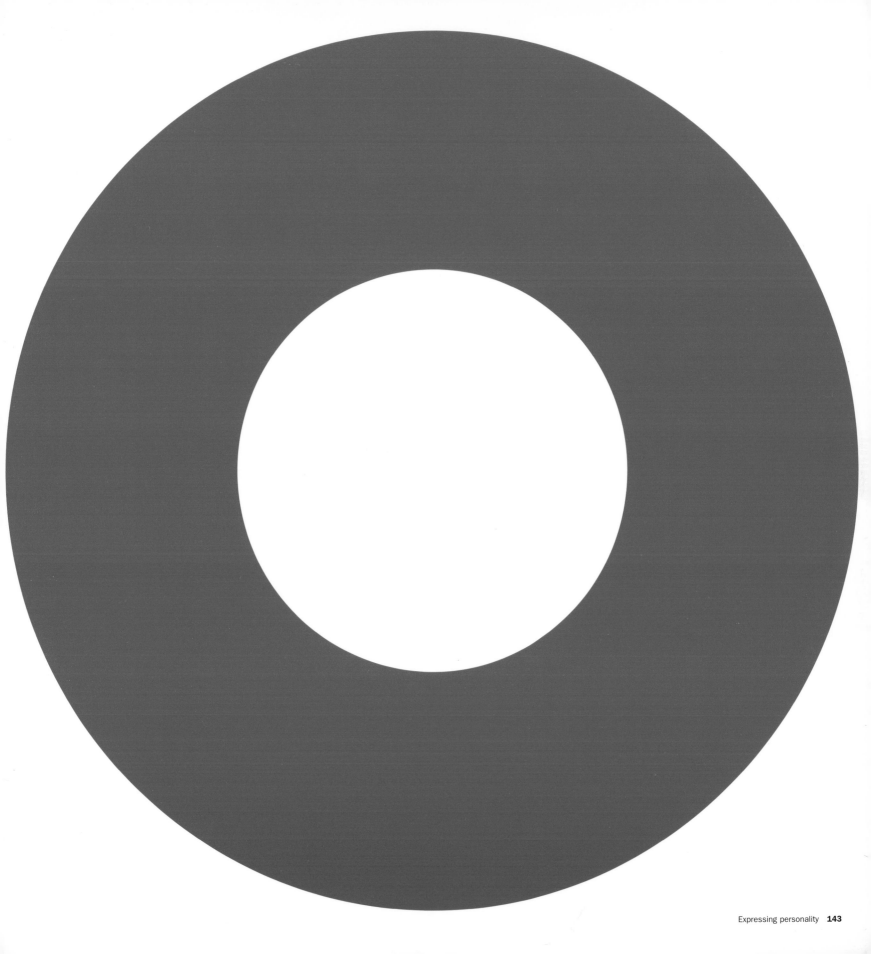

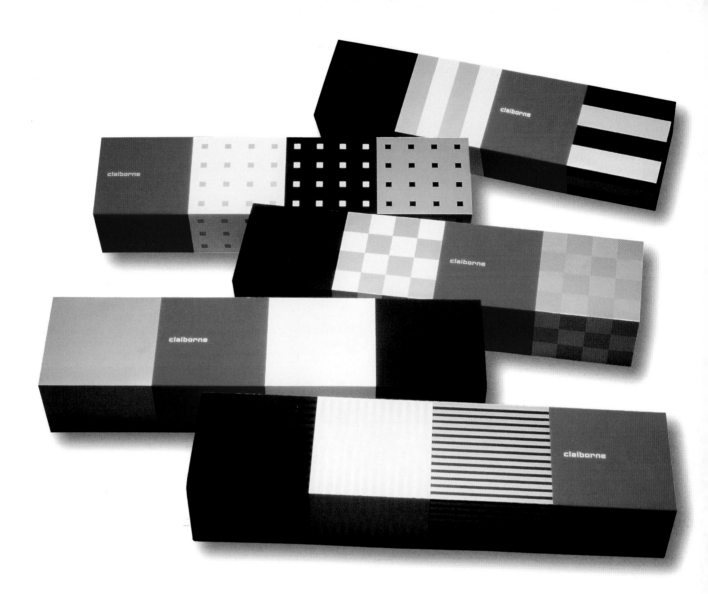

Establishing a personality for a scent has more to do with packaging than chemistry. The look and treatment reflect the target audience.

A series of graphic and tactile elements borrowed from a "man's world"—black rubber and frosted glass, striped shirts and pin-striped suits, a brilliant red cube—establish a bold, strong, masculine motif for a new men's fragrance line. Using these limited elements in a variety of combinations, with minimal identification graphics, maintains a clear, distinct personality through a range of bottles, gift packages, and displays.

Geometric shapes, unusual color combinations, triangular bottles, tactile materials, shapes rotated 15°— all help forge a distinct personality for a large range of fragrances, toiletries, and accessories marketed by Liz Claiborne for women.

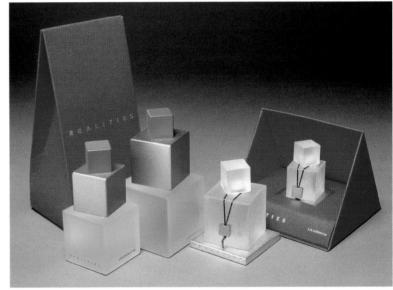

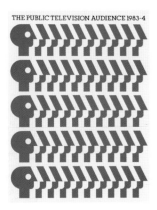

THE PUBLIC TELEVISION AUDIENCE 1983-4

When it comes to expressing personality, *how* depends on *who*. Sometimes a bit of wit is called for. A sense of fun can be the difference between an identity that is memorable and one that is merely recognizable.

The PBS (Public Broadcasting Service) mark uses a stylized profile of the human face, based on the letter "P." Similar to the initial letterform of a previous PBS logo, it repeats the profile three times, playfully putting the "public," in public television.

For Andrew McMeel Universal, a publisher of humor and self-improvement books, cards, and calendars, adding two dots to the initial "U" for Universal turns the letterform into a face. By carefully determining the size of the eyes and the width of the nose, the design gives the mark a chameleon-like quality that makes it equally at home on a serious publication or a humorous one.

"The measure of success is not whether you have a tough problem to deal with, but whether it's the same problem you had last year." John Foster Dulles

GEMINI.®

Comedians call it a running gag. Composers call it a leit-motif. But whether you're aiming for slapstick humor or grand opera, the premise is the same: consistent use of a few bold elements can establish a recognizable personality. This holds true in graphics as well.

For a management consulting firm that wanted to clearly distinguish itself from its more conservative competition, a system of highlighting key phrases of text, applied to brochures and advertising, relies on a simple but consistent graphic approach to set the company apart in a variety of situations.

Establishing a graphic personality for an art museum provides a splendid opportunity for the designer; a chance to harness the fundamental elements of art.

For the Museum of Contemporary Art (MOCA) in Los Angeles, the graphic identity combines the basic geometric forms of design— the square, the circle, and the triangle—with the letter C. These shapes also become a thread running through a series of invitations, greeting cards, brochures, and other materials. For MOCA's interim location in a converted warehouse, known as the Temporary Contemporary, a handwritten "t" was inserted into the museum's basic logotype to convey the idea of "temporary."

The Toledo Museum of Art called for a very different look. Here, an open square suggests a picture frame, certainly an appropriate allusion for an art museum. In print, the museum name becomes part of the picture space within. The effect makes the logo an open frame, allowing imagery, colors and textures to show through.

Knoll, a leading manufacturer of contemporary furniture, has always stood for excellence in design. But some of its luster dimmed when a series of corporate mergers seemed to water down the firm's focus on fine design.

In the early 1990s, new owners determined to reinvigorate Knoll's reputation. A bold logo-type was reestablished, and a strong graphic personality developed. The concept of overlapping images, applied to a broad range of printed materials from catalogs to graphics guidelines and giveaway items, made a bold statement about a company reclaiming its heritage and philosophy.

The Knoll Group
Identity Guidelines

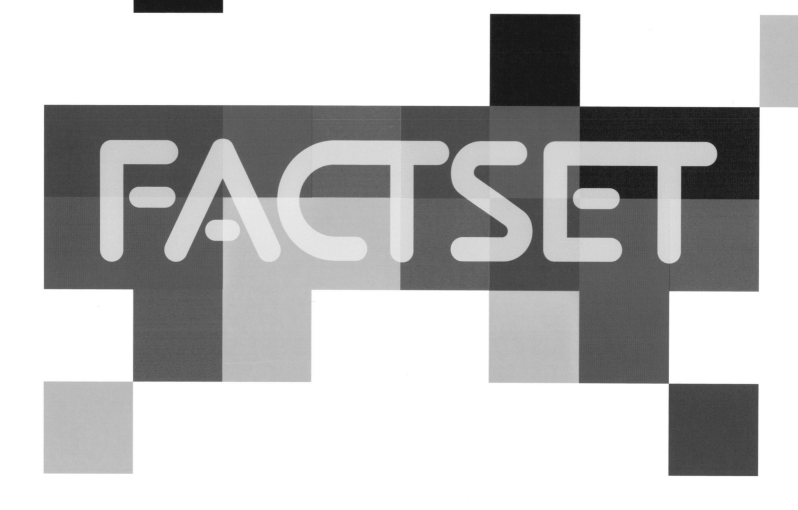

Looking to maximize
your investment
performance?

You don't need
more sources of
financial information.

FactSet Research Systems Inc. uses sophisticated online systems to provide financial institutions with up-to-the-minute data on financial markets and analytical resources.

To express the vibrant nature of this young company, and to suggest that it brings together in one place a vast array of information, a graphic treatment paired a bold logotype with a palette of bright colors and applied them across a broad range of printed materials.

A series of promotional pieces highlight this distinctive character. One brochure uses a toy car, painted in the FactSet colors, to make its point. A series of seemingly unrelated parts come together to form a complete automobile.

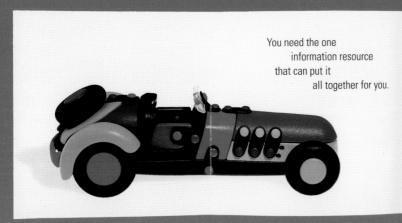

You need the one
information resource
that can put it
all together for you.

FACTSET

To enhance your investment performance, you need an information resource that's more than the sum of its parts. Many services offer a wide array of databases. But only the FactSet online service offers you the tools to integrate this global information totally and seamlessly, turning raw data from more than 50 different databases into usable, actionable investment intelligence.

FactSet has been helping institutional investors make information meaningful since 1978. Our proprietary software is the result of over 15 years of dialogue between FactSet and thousands of FactSet clients—from investment bankers to research analysts to portfolio managers. Using FactSet software, you can easily cull information from multiple databases into a single report. Or set up multi-database screening systems. Or integrate your own proprietary data into our system. In short, you can custom-tailor vast amounts of financial data to meet your personal information needs 24 hours a day, 365 days a year.

To learn more about how you can integrate a world of investment information, and turn financial information into financial intelligence, please call Philip Hadley at 203.863.1500.

Visit us on the World Wide Web at
http://www.factset.com

NBC
SPORTS

NBC
ENTERPRISES

Date

Date

From

From

To

NBC
RADIO

30 Rockefeller Plaza
New York, NY 10020
212 664 4444

National
Broadcasting
Company, Inc.

Date

NBC

NBC
TV STATIONS

NBC
ENTERTAINMENT

Date

From

To

112 West Center
Fayetteville, AR 72701
501 443 2400

KPOM-TV
4624 Kelley Highway
P.O. Box 1867
Fort Smith, AR 72902
501 785 2400

24 ﷯ KPOM-TV
FORT SMITH

NBC
TV NETWORK

Date

1957

1975

1980

Television bombards viewers
with an endless stream of
images and impressions. To
burst through the visual
mayhem, a TV network needs
a bold graphic identity. This
visual presence also must be
distinctive enough to hold
its own through innumerable
variations and animations,
reflecting the range of
programming that is part of
24-hour broadcasting.

Decades back, when NBC
first made the transition from
black-and-white to color
television, an illustration of a
peacock, a colorful bird
fond of strutting its plumage,
symbolized the network's
new palette. Over the years,
the plucky bird endured in
various forms.

The challenge for NBC, over
time, was how to retain the
beloved peacock, yet turn it
into a powerful graphic symbol
rather than an illustration.
A redesign simplified the bird's
form, slimming it down to
six equally shaped feathers
in a rainbow of primary broadcast colors.

Designed in 1979, but not
released until 1985, the
reborn NBC peacock logo has
become one of the world's
most highly recognized marks.

Teaching through play
Creating playful, interactive learning experiences

Poor Jack. His famous regimen of "all work and no play" makes him a dull boy. Or so we're told. But the adage is a bit misleading. It supposes a sharp distinction between work and play. Where kids are concerned (and perhaps adults, too), work and play are intimately entwined. Play is the medium through which children experience the world around them. It is how they experiment with ideas, objects, environments, and relationships.

There are many meanings of "play," of course. A play on words, for instance, reveals subtle connections and hidden meanings.

The notion of teaching through play leads us to create environments in which children learn by doing. Complex concepts do not demand complex presentations. We can explore sophisticated ideas through approachable activities, through playful activities that make the abstract real.

By tapping into the child in all of us that likes to play and explore, a very participatory outdoor exhibit at the Children's Museum of Manhattan teaches kids the values of conservation: recycling, rethinking, and reusing. In an area devoted to the amount of water city dwellers need and use, and exploring where that water comes from, a hand-cranked pump and mist create a mini water world. It's a novel environment that can be visually and intellectually challenging— and really, really refreshing on a sticky summer day.

The structure of the museum's Urban Tree House incorporates safety cones on the water tank, barricade striping on the fences, and other reminders of the urban visual environment.

As part of the effort to teach recycling, the Children's Museum of Manhattan invites kids to collect and bring in plastic bottles from home. The kids then craft the bottles into flying creatures. The best are strung up on wires and changed on a weekly basis.

This hands-on activity lets children join the design process. Along the way, they learn something about the idea of reuse as an effective means of conservation, with exciting graphic results.

EVE MERRIAM

THE HOLE STORY

DESIGNED AND ILLUSTRATED BY
IVAN CHERMAYEFF

Holes are meant to be filled, plugged, poked, or looked through. Blanks and incomplete images are invitations to fill in the missing pieces and complete the image.

The Hole Story is a children's book. It begins with holes in the cover itself, encouraging small kids to use the book as a mask, or to poke fingers through and give the mouth teeth or make funny eyes. More participation equals more fun…and maybe more reading.

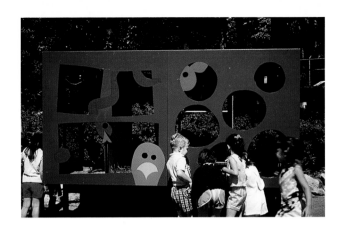

At the St. Louis Children's Zoo, cages for small animals use graphic panels to protect them from the sun. Viewing holes offer an engaging way to peek inside at the animals.

In a series of freestanding panels set up along one of the zoo's walkways, the roles are reversed. Here, kids don't look in holes to see animals... they look in holes to *become* animals, or at least part of the display by completing an animal's face or nose. Of course, the kids can't see themselves, but they *can* enjoy the process. And the parents enjoy a great photo opportunity.

kidpower

Playgrounds are superb environments for teaching through play. Children have fun discovering and experimenting without being aware of the learning process, without knowing that they are gathering experiences.

A long blue line becomes a thread running through Kidpower, a 30,000-square-foot playground at the New York Hall of Science. Off the blue line, kids learn about physics by using slides, climbing nets, weight lifting, and much else. Sound parabolas let them talk to each other in a whisper from one end of the playground to the other. Bright colors, soft surfaces to fall on, water, sound, and movement all contribute to an environment where kids learn stuff without feeling as if they're in school.

On a sign near the entrance, a motorized dot over the "i" in Kidpower's logotype swings up to the top of the "d" every few seconds. The notion of "power" becomes more than just a word in the name. The visible action makes it reality.

Curiosity is a powerful force. (We all know what it did to that cat!) Revealing something in part drives people to uncover the whole.

At "Science City," a temporary exhibit in the middle of Manhattan's Herald Square, various devices allow New Yorkers and visitors alike to look down into underground electric connections or subways and sewers, or to peer up at communication towers, rooftop antennas, and floodlighting. Observation of these everyday, yet often unnoticed, systems helps people understand the complexity of keeping a big city working, moving, and connected.

POWERED BY KIDS
COMMINS?
GEAR?

Kids' creative energies can be set free by giving them unexpected materials to work with, then letting their imagination take over.

At Kidscommons in Columbus, Indiana, local manufacturers provided a continual flow of product components and left-over materials. These became the raw materials for the children's creative activities.

In the same town, the kids' day-care center at a diesel engine plant is identified by a logo with playfully interlocking letter-form gears.

The language of play can explain important subjects in ways that are both sympathetic and approachable. Play doesn't have to mean child's play either; fun and games can lead to clear understanding for young and old.

At Expo '70 in Osaka, Japan, children could experience first-hand what it is like to sit in an astronaut's seat.

The game of Monopoly teaches us the value of money, real estate, luck, risk-taking, and social skills, among other things. So does this "Productivity" board game, devised as a take-home item for visitors to a Smithsonian Institution exhibition. Playing the game by using everyday markers—coins, candy, keys, bottle caps, etc.— each player advances or retreats as the dice and the board command. By the time this chutes-and-ladders-like game is over, the player has understood the fundamental points raised in the exhibition.

An annual report cover for Irwin Financial features a sequence of mathematical signs leading to the company's "i" logo.

To connect all the parties involved in the education process, Cablevision created a high-speed Internet system for students, teachers, and parents. Called Power to Learn, it provides a valuable learning resource, connecting 500,000 students, 15,000 schools, and 500 libraries to its broadband network. The logo is a colorful star made of rotating check marks—the traditional symbol of approval, correctness, and achievement. The powerful graphic is the cornerstone of an identity program that sets the tone for diverse print and web applications.

As we teach through play, we also can say serious things with good humor and tongue firmly in cheek. The 60-second presentation shown at the right was delivered at a 1995 AIGA design conference, exploring the theme of "Love, Money, Power."

Voice over:

After staring at the words this ONE jumped out at me. No matter how you look at it, it's only ONE minute!

If you flush it left, LOVE is short; however, MONEY & POWER are justified. OOOEEE!

If you put LOVE between MONEY & POWER you get a better rag!

If LOVE is bigger than MONEY & POWER it's all justified.

If POWER is condensed, your LOVE overextended, and MONEY is short and tight, you're probably trying too hard.

If you take LOVE, MONEY, and POWER and flush it right, it all will go down the toilet.

Delighting audiences
Building audience anticipation

To be able to excite and seduce
an audience—to make a child laugh, to
enthrall an adult, to make people
draw connections to their own lives—
is a designer's dream. It's not easy
to do all this in a poster, an invitation,
or a mailing piece. After all, the designer
isn't putting on the show, but simply
providing a taste of a future performance,
program, or party. To design for the
performing arts is a challenge because
one cannot make the audience see,
hear, or touch. A poster is a promise.

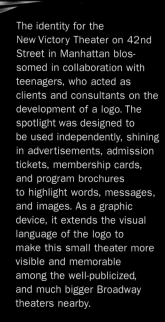

The identity for the
New Victory Theater on 42nd
Street in Manhattan blos-
somed in collaboration with
teenagers, who acted as
clients and consultants on the
development of a logo. The
spotlight was designed to
be used independently, shining
in advertisements, admission
tickets, membership cards,
and program brochures
to highlight words, messages,
and images. As a graphic
device, it extends the visual
language of the logo to
make this small theater more
visible and memorable
among the well-publicized,
and much bigger Broadway
theaters nearby.

In entertainment arenas, identity is not an end in and of itself. Symbols are subservient to the shows or events unfolding there. Crafting a character is more about attitude and feeling, helping to tie together a diverse program of performances while nurturing an audience's positive feelings and sense of participation.

Sometimes design doesn't just reflect its subject, but actually shapes its subject. The image of a baby elephant balancing on a ball and juggling the letters that spell Big Apple Circus was captivating enough to encourage Paul Binder, the ringmaster and circus owner, to go out and purchase a baby elephant. The next year, the circus adopted a "western" theme and the image became that of a baby elephant astride a buffalo. The circus bought a baby buffalo. The power of images does not usually bring about such dramatic results.

For the Fox Theatres chain, the company's logotype becomes a background for the popcorn and soda packaging, adding a sense of quality rather than simply blaring an advertisement.

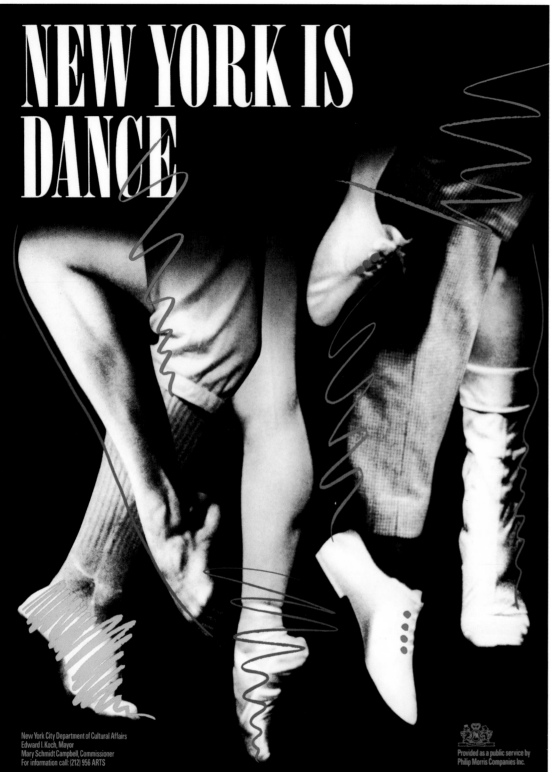

NEW YORK IS DANCE

New York City Department of Cultural Affairs
Edward I. Koch, Mayor
Mary Schmidt Campbell, Commissioner
For information call: (212) 956 ARTS

Provided as a public service by
Philip Morris Companies Inc.

New York and the Arts: A Cultural Affair ⚡Martha Graham Dance Company ⚡Joffrey Ballet ⚡Lar Lubovitch ⚡PS.122 ⚡Merce Cunningham ⚡BCBC ⚡Eli Wagoner ⚡Rod Rodgers ⚡Dinizulu and his African Dancers ⚡David Gordon/Pickup Performance Company ⚡Paul Taylor Dance Company ⚡Dancewave/Diane ncers ⚡Trisha Brown ⚡New York City Ballet ⚡Bill T. Jones/Arnie Zane ⚡Jubilation! ⚡Laura Dean ⚡Asian American Dance Theatre ⚡Joyce Theater ⚡Eiko and e Gonzalez ⚡Limon Dance Company ⚡Nikolais Dance Company ⚡Alvin Ailey American Dance Theater ⚡Lucinda Childs Dance Company ⚡Meredith Monk/Th mon ⚡Ballet Hispanico ⚡Erick Hawkins ⚡Murray Louis Dance Company ⚡Feld Ballet ⚡American Ballet Theatre ⚡Saeko Ichinohe and Company ⚡Bronx Dan Driver and Harry ⚡Dance Theater Workshop ⚡Eleo Pomare ⚡Chen & Dancers ⚡City Center Theater ⚡Dance Theatre of Harlem ⚡and much, much more...

Design is cumulative. The more one sees of the parts, the more one understands the whole.

The New York City Department of Cultural Affairs wanted to inform visitors to the city about Gotham's many rich cultural attractions.

A nine-part poster series took this message to all the major points of entry: airports, train stations, and information centers. Each poster suggests a range of options within each broad cultural category such as music, history, museums, and art. The participating institutions are listed at the bottom of each poster. The result was a series of independent pieces, each of which celebrated some aspect of New York culture, and all of which together suggested the city's staggering array of choices.

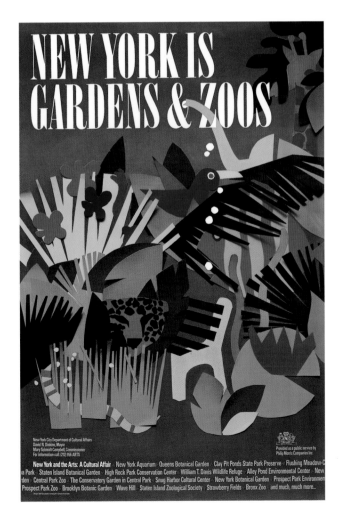

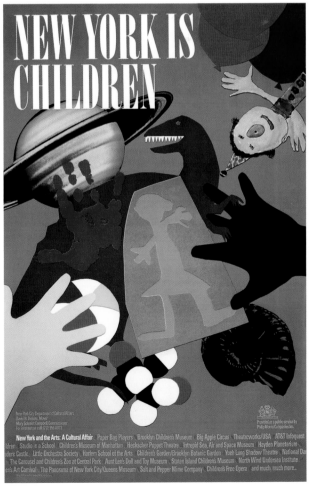

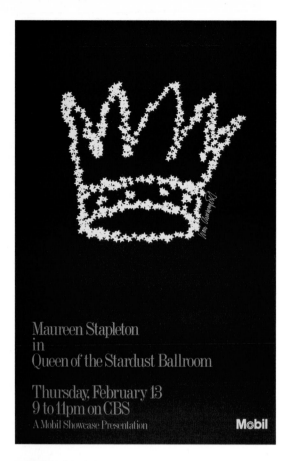

Maureen Stapleton
in
Queen of the Stardust Ballroom

Thursday, February 13
9 to 11pm on CBS
A Mobil Showcase Presentation

Mobil

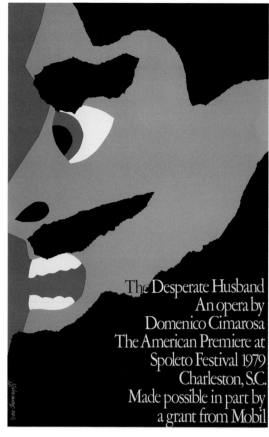

The Desperate Husband
An opera by
Domenico Cimarosa
The American Premiere at
Spoleto Festival 1979
Charleston, S.C.
Made possible in part by
a grant from Mobil

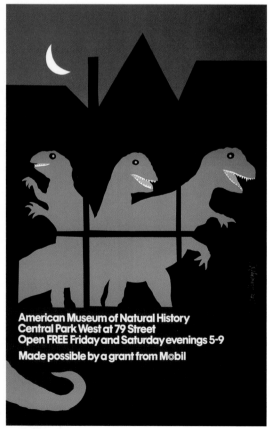

American Museum of Natural History
Central Park West at 79 Street
Open FREE Friday and Saturday evenings 5–9

Made possible by a grant from Mobil

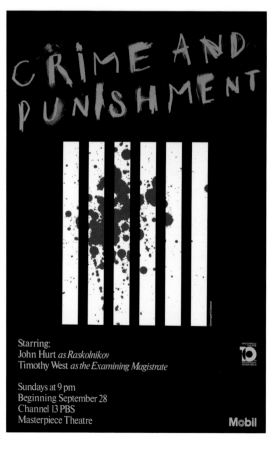

CRIME AND PUNISHMENT

Starring:
John Hurt *as Raskolnikov*
Timothy West *as the Examining Magistrate*

Sundays at 9 pm
Beginning September 28
Channel 13 PBS
Masterpiece Theatre

Mobil

An unread book will never have an impact on a reader. An unheard idea will never intrigue a listener. Before a design can delight an audience, it must first draw an audience.

In the entertainment world, posters and advertisements usually are placed in very competitive environments. Ads jostle for space in the entertainment section of newspapers, each screaming for attention. Posters hang in heavily trafficked, visually demanding spots. The first challenge, therefore, is simply to be noticed. How? As Monty Python famously put it, "And now for something completely different."

The crown belongs to the "Queen of the Stardust Ballroom." It was made by drawing with glue and sprinkling the drawing with sequins.

For the Spoleto Festival, the larger-than-life husband is so outraged that his nose pokes beyond the poster.

On Friday and Saturday evenings at the American Museum of Natural History, the dinosaurs are at home to visitors.

Crime and Punishment puts the blood splatter of crime behind bars. The title is crudely chalked onto the prison wall.

The image of man is composed from fragments of Einstein, a Masai tribesman, a businessman, a classical sculpture, and other facial images. Together, they embody the grand sweep of Jacob Bronowski's milestone 1975 TV series on the pivotal points of man's evolution.

The
Ascent
of
Man

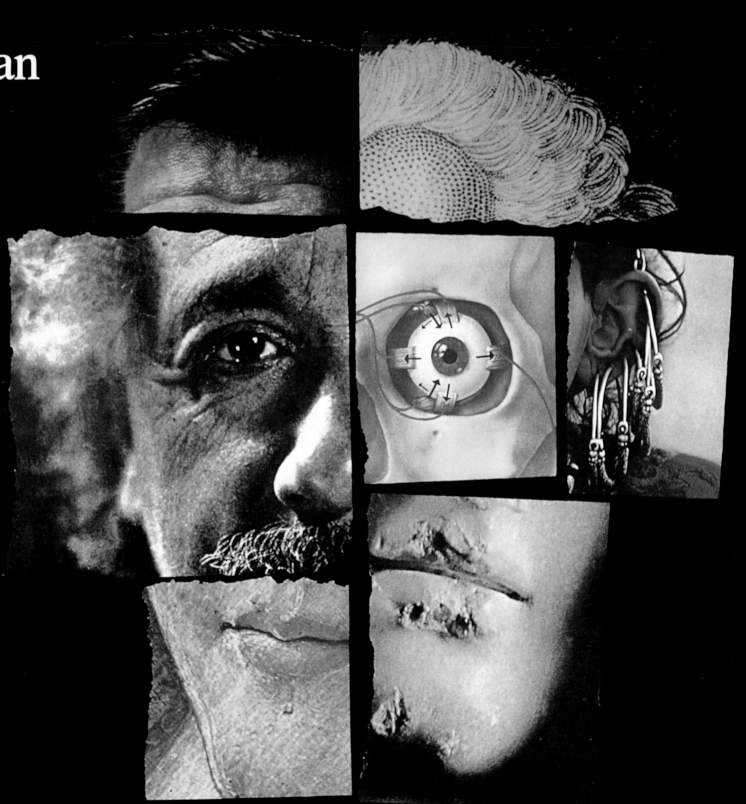

Hartford
Ballet
presents
The
Nutcracker

December
15-18

Bushnell
Hall

For tickets
call
246-6807

Thanks to United Technologies for this message

To delight audiences, design
can elicit the connected feelings of festivity, good spirits,
and joy. Evoking those feelings
can charm people, putting
them in a frame of mind to
be enchanted.

For the Hartford Ballet, a
merry band of images from
The Nutcracker—a Christmas
tree, a Russian dancer, and
a toy soldier—come together
to form a single festive fellow.
Buttons and eyes, bells,
and holiday ornaments are the
dots holding together the
exuberant collage.

37th New York

Film Festival Sept. 24 – Oct. 10, 1999

Alice Tully Hall

Presented by the Film Society of Lincoln Center

The 37th New York Film Festival is sponsored by *Grand Marnier* and, in part, with public funds from the New York State Council on the Arts.

Overlapping strips of film let loose their sprocket holes in a blizzard of cascading confetti to celebrate the Film Society of Lincoln Center.

World's Fair. The very name calls to mind grand possibilities —an unparalleled chance to captivate the public. Fairs offer the opportunity to present images and ideas in new ways using new technology. The potential is boundless.

"The Louisiana Story" at the state pavilion at Expo '84 in New Orleans provided an occasion to remember the past, the land, the people, the voices, the music, and the food. Thousands of visitors took an indoor boat ride of the fair's home state, through the bayous, landscapes, and architecture of Louisiana, culminating with floats, sounds, and images of Mardi Gras, resplendent with outlandish costumes. The ride left visitors exhilarated and feeling good about Louisiana and the fair.

I've been through The Mill

Movement attracts attention. It doesn't much matter whether the viewer moves, or the design moves...or both.

The Mill at Burlington Industries at Sixth Avenue and 54th Street in New York delivered one basic message: "The textile industry isn't as boring as you think it is." A moving walkway took thousands of visitors daily through a simulated textile mill, with its whirring and spinning machinery, its related noise, movement, and steam. The three-story-high space was clad with mirrors to expand the illusion and multiply the movement, suggesting a vast textile mill.

After passing the simulated mill, the sidewalk carried visitors into a dimly lighted area where, to a score by the Kinks, rapidly changing images from 76 projectors formed seemingly random combinations of clothes and types of people. The underlying message was that textiles are woven into the fabric of American life.

The street-level windows of The Mill were enlivened by a colorful quilt-like collage of fabrics.

Every visitor received a souvenir button verifying that they had indeed been through The Mill.

Gathering and collecting
Transforming the ordinary into the extraordinary

E Pluribus Unum—out of many, one. It's the slogan of the United States. It could easily be the maxim of the designer who combines images, objects, or varied materials to create something singular, something distinct from the sum of its parts.

A collection unites related objects, which then take on special character and meaning. Both the common bonds and the diversity of objects give collections a new voice and a new force. Designers can harness the power of the patterns that lie dormant in any grouping of related objects— not just patterns of texture, color, and material, but also patterns of association in the eye of the viewer.

Shopkeepers recognized long ago that massive piles of fruits and vegetables in grocery stores or neat rows of coffee mugs in housewares departments are more alluring than any single orange or tomato or mug can ever hope to be. Designers can also make use of this phenomenon.

IBM has a presence in many countries around the world. And those countries, in turn, have a presence on the walls of IBM's World Trade Americas headquarters in White Plains, New York, where colorful collections of everyday stuff from 27 nations is used as artwork throughout the building. Each piece is a collection of one category of things that everyone would recognize and understand such as coffee beans, ribbons, toys, seed packages, and postage stamps. Arranged by color or other visual characteristic, the items are placed in a series of square, clear Plexiglas boxes, which in turn are arranged in modular grids.

For visitors and employees alike, the collections carry a lively message of internationalism.

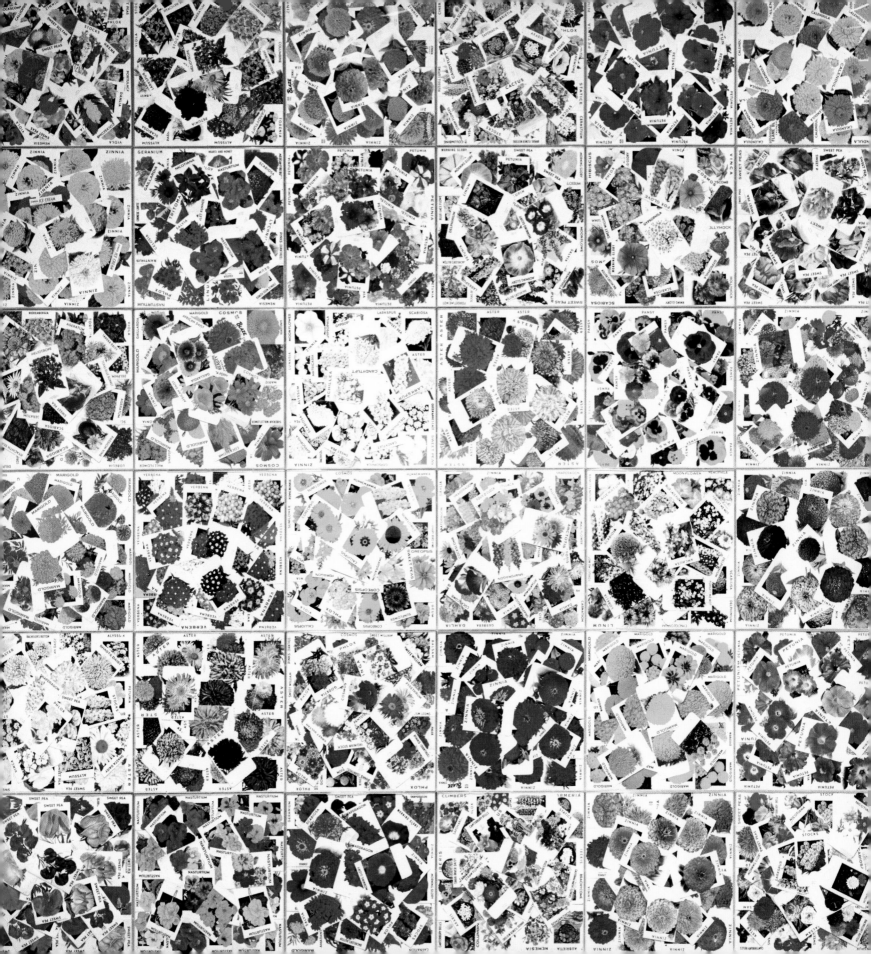

In the company's stand-up cafeteria, a 30-foot-long display is a grid of clear box frames, each containing miniature national flags from one of 130 countries.

In many collections, "happy accidents" are part of the charm and beauty. The idea plants the seed, which quickly takes on a life of its own. Making precise arrangements within the grid boxes was unnecessary. The only consideration that mattered was specifying the best size box for the material, then standing back to watch the collection grow.

⊞ EDGEWOOD a comprehensive collection designed for executive and public spaces by architect William Armbruster

FOR NEW CATALOG WRITE EDGEWOOD, 334 EAST 75TH STREET, NEW YORK 21, NEW YORK

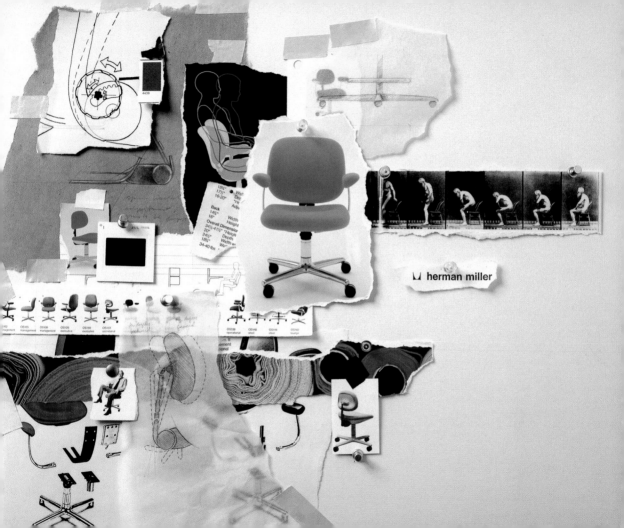

herman miller

SANDRA DAY O'CONNOR
UNITED STATES COURTHOUSE

Phoenix, Arizona

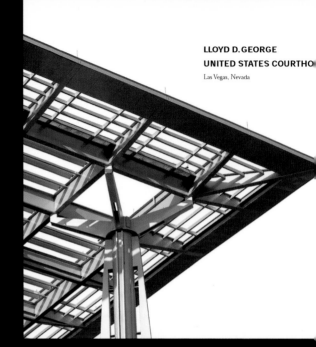

**LLOYD D. GEORGE
UNITED STATES COURTHO**

Las Vegas, Nevada

Sometimes a piece of a
picture can be more intriguing
than the entire picture. Even
a hint of an image may be
enough to express the whole.

A series of brochures on design
excellence in the architecture
of federal courthouses highlights building parts instead of
using more conventional facade
shots. The result focuses the
viewer's eye on telling details
while creating a dramatic interplay of forms.

**UNITED STATES COURTHOUSE
AND FEDERAL BUILDING**

Central Islip, New York

Rhythm & BLU. John Blake, Didier Lockwood, Michael Urbaniak.

While searching for a way to capture the feeling of the music on this Gramavision LP, the designers arranged pieces of cut paper on a drawing table...until it was noticed that the discarded cuttings on the floor were more interesting than the arrangement on the drawing board. Presto, and the scraps became the design, immediately collected and photographed.

The idea for the image used on a catalog cover and invitation for an annual report competition arises from the observation that when the reports are stacked up, the spines reveal various colors and patterns, different in each individual case but adding up to a fresh look at annual reports.

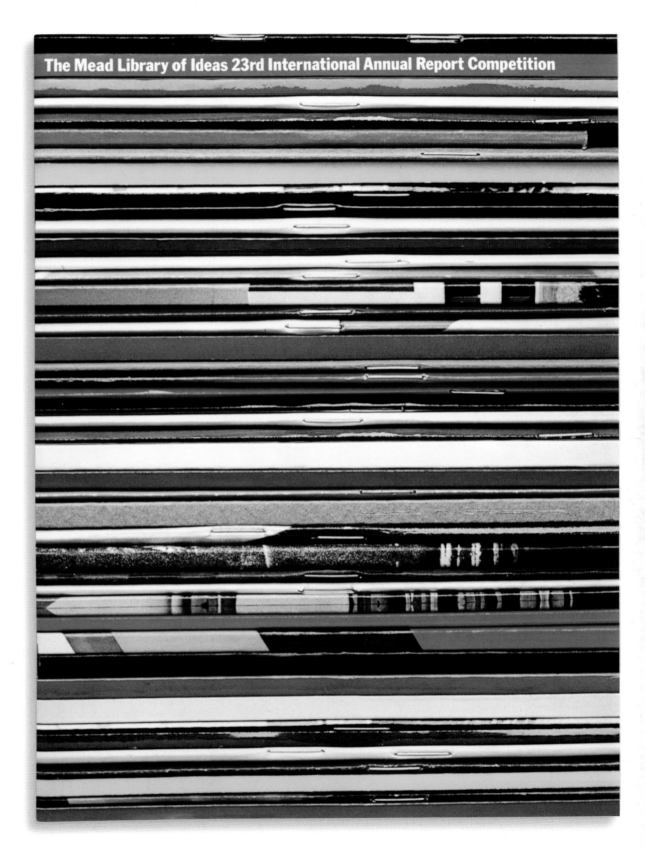

The Mead Library of Ideas 23rd International Annual Report Competition

DESTINATION MIA

HOTEL MIA

As Yogi Berra once said, "You observe a lot by looking." The discoveries that come from seeing and recognizing opportunities is an essential part of a designer's modus operandi.

MIA is the airport code for Miami International Airport. This led to the name Hotel MIA to identify the hotel located in the center of the airport terminal. The abbreviation grew from a simple observation. And it not only put a crisp ID in place of a cumbersome name, but created a particularly appropriate dual meaning as well. Many of the airport visitors and hotel guests are Hispanic and thus read "Hotel MIA" as "my hotel."

The renaming, and this ad, takes full advantage of the fact that no matter where you're flying from, your Miami-bound luggage will always say MIA on the tag. So everyone arriving by air unknowingly becomes a walking promotion.

Another use of airline baggage tags as evocative symbols revealed how much information the tags in fact contain. The three letters on every tag are shorthand for destinations worldwide; coded keys to a vast transportation network… and an essential part of the system that directs the right bags to the right planes (most of the time). Color coding the tags helps the process as well, as does keeping them the same size, regardless of the airline carrier.

This poster was distributed to schools by the International Design Conference in Aspen. Its message to students? That different situations and different tasks require different methods and languages of communication.

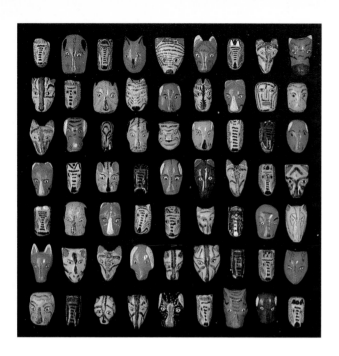

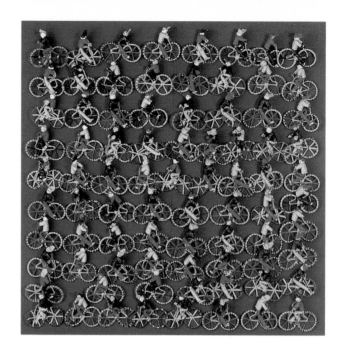

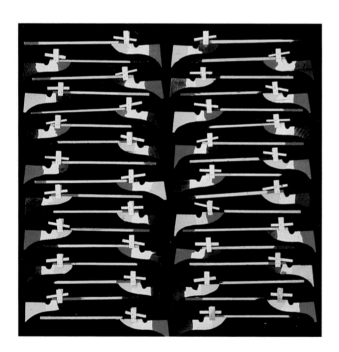

Multiply an object or image and you often multiply viewer interest. Just one of anything can be a bit dull. A cavalcade of the same thing can be riveting.

Hand-painted toys bought on the streets of Mexico City decorate the local offices of Mobil Oil. In quantity, the toys become increasingly magical.

Dozens of boxers, gaggles of whistles, prides of pistols, clutches of dolls are assembled together to form visually exciting wall displays. The frames cost more than the toys.

The final result was so enchanting that the Mexican government borrowed the display and dispatched it as a traveling exhibition to Europe.

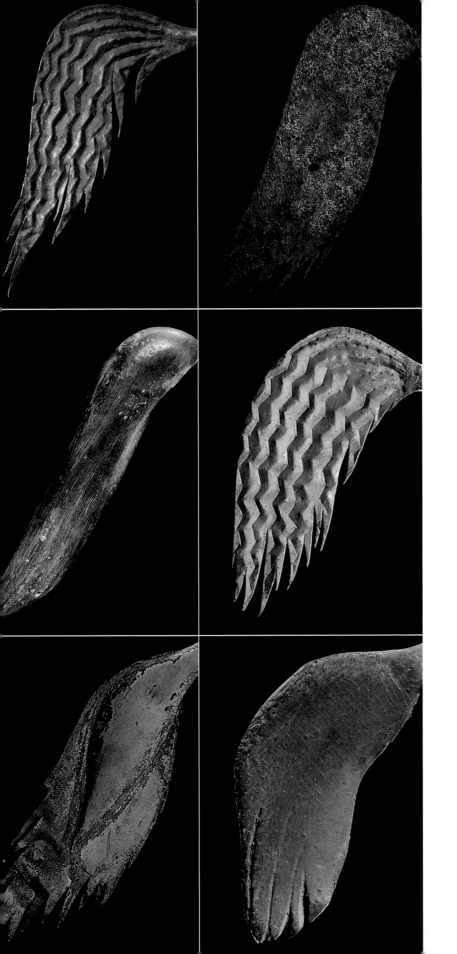

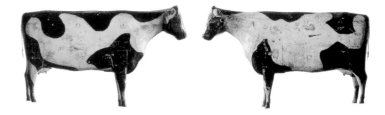

"God is in the details," observed Mies van der Rohe. Beauty, interest, and meaning sometimes reside there too. Focusing on a single detail can dramatize the range of materials, textures and forms that thrive in a single category of objects or a single setting.

In this case, horses' tails reveal the incredible diversity within a single collection of American weathervanes which, along with the wooden cow above, are included in the book *Spiritually Moving*.

People often can recognize the whole from just a fragment of an image or word.

A book of posters by a variety of artists and designers commissioned by Mobil Corporation was given a cover that featured overlapping layers of the lower left-hand corner of a few of the posters. This teasing hint of some of the memorable examples— and the implication of hidden riches just beyond view— reminds readers of the innumerable highly publicized programs supported by Mobil

The poster for a lecture on the importance of drawing depicts fragments of work falling out of the designer's portfolio. The bits tantalize; a peek piques interest.

Posters made possible by a grant from Mobil

A collection of 250 international posters commissioned by Mobil and selected by The Poster Society

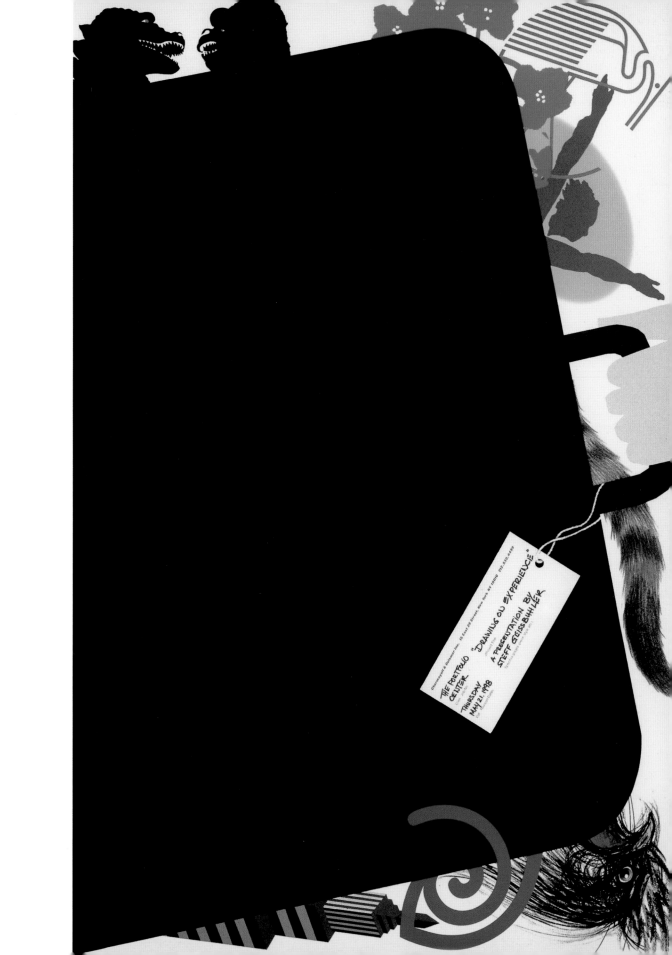

THE PORTFOLIO CENTER

"DRAWING ON EXPERIENCE"

A PRESENTATION BY
STEFF GEISSBUHLER

THURSDAY
MAY 21, 1998

Collecting often celebrates differences rather than commonality. A bouquet is a collection that, in its combinations, creates a symphony of variations through a common theme.

An array of fishes evokes choice on a menu cover of an elegant seafood restaurant in Rockefeller Center.

To encourage saving money, each year Savings Day is celebrated in Germany. This poster was made for the day and collecting generally. Specimen bags pinned to a board contain liquids, insects, stamps, coins, and other ephemera to suggest the wide range of things that are collectible—and savable.

For a catalog cover of an exhibit on the state of drawing, details from the work of the 26 artists in the show are featured in the order in which they appear in the Museum of Modern Art exhibition.

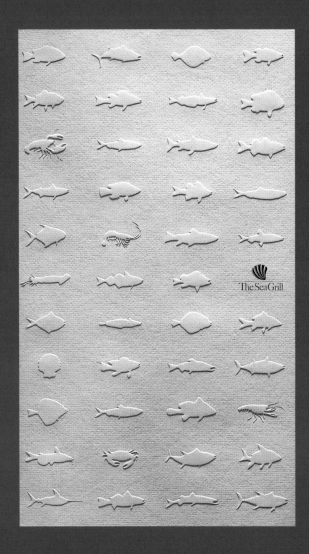

drawing now.

eight propositions

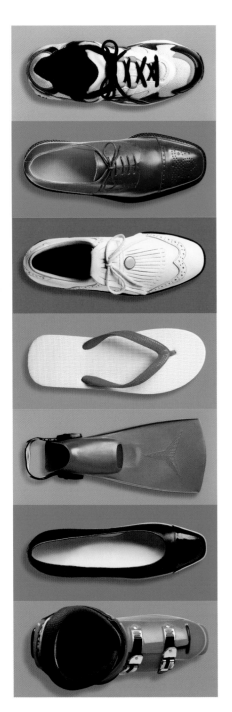

A collection can be like a mirror: more meaningful for the activities or ideas it reflects than for its actual contents.

The Marriott Rewards program rewards its members and frequent hotel guests with free vacation trips to its many hotels around the globe. Different sorts of footwear reflect a variety of vacation possibilities —from beach to golf, from snorkeling to skiing—associating the rewards with travel, vacation, and leisure activities *without* resorting to the obvious landscapes or travel photos. Other images in the series included collections of luggage and hats.

One wall of the American Center on Productivity is concerned with American workers' contribution to the economy. Hats symbolize their many and varied professions, including welders, fisherman, bakers, farmers, construction workers, and all the services—fire and police, soldiers and sailors, nurses and doctors—collected and arranged in the niches of a two-story-high space.

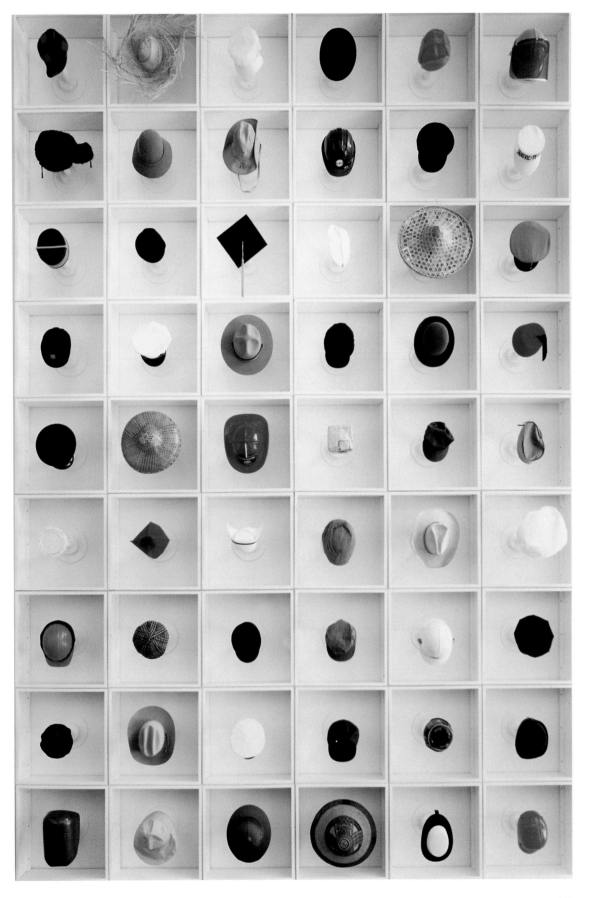

From pinstripes and diamonds to bats and balls, baseball nurtures a rich visual language all its own. The equipment, the uniforms, and the spoken language are unique. They also are instantly evocative of deeply rooted traditions and values.

A series of themed collections enlivens the public halls and stairwells of Major League Baseball's headquarters. Each represents a different aspect of the sport. Sorting these items into groups or organizing them in cases makes it possible to see the objects— and the history they represent —in new contexts.

Gathering and collecting is not the exclusive province of designers. Just ask the fellow with the album of stamps or the kid with 700 neatly organized bottle caps. Or the Library of Congress.

Congress established the institution in 1800. Twelve years later, the British burned its building to the ground. Thomas Jefferson, determined to reestablish the collection, sold Congress his renowned personal library of over 6,000 volumes. To celebrate the institution's bicentennial in 2000, the Library of Congress reconstituted Jefferson's original collection, gathering replacements where necessary.

Large wood and glass cases, designed and arranged in a spiral form, displayed the entire collection, with the books visible from both sides. A computerized index lets visitors locate any volume in the collection...a convenience Jefferson probably would have appreciated.

Jefferson's Library

Shifting scale
Manipulating size to attract attention

"'What a curious feeling!' said Alice, 'I must be shutting up like a telescope.'" Poor Alice. To shrink and to grow she had to rely on a potion labeled "DRINK ME" and a cake with "EAT ME" spelled out neatly in black currants. We can change size (or at least seem to change size) more easily, simply by shifting scale. But the result is much the same: surprise, impact, and a fresh perspective. As in the famous Charles and Ray Eames film, *Powers of 10*—and for Alice—playing with scale alters our viewpoint, compelling us to look and think again.

Playing with scale lets the designer focus and direct a viewer's attention, giving impact to what might otherwise have been overlooked. It transforms the common into the uncommon, altering the relationship between the viewer and the viewed.

A venerable saying advises, "If in doubt, make it red. If *still* in doubt, make it big."

The "Flying Red O" at Mobil Oil headquarters in Fairfax, Virginia, and the 32-foot-high "O Tower" for Mobil's largest research center near Princeton, New Jersey, are perfect examples of both.

Art and design are modes of expression. But the master of expression, of course, is the human face. Enlarged and closely cropped, it almost always projects a powerful image.

During renovation of an office building facing Madison Square Park in New York City, an etching of President James Madison, the man for whom the square was named, was painted directly on plywood. Looking from across the park, Madison's visage took on a photographic likeness. Up close, the image became completely abstract. Panels of trivia revealed interesting and little-known facts about him and his presidency, such as Dolley Madison introducing ice cream to the White House.

In a poster for the Metropolitan Museum of Art, reduced type size increases the sense of scale, making Alexander the Great even greater.

At the Liberty Island Museum, visitors have the rare chance to confront the Statue of Liberty face to face. Accurate, full-size copper replicas of the statue's face and foot —fabricated with the original tools and by the same crafts-men who renovated the statue in 1986—dramatize the scale and power of the work.

Perspective is powerful. Everyday objects, when enlarged to unusual dimensions, take on a completely different aspect.

At Turning Stone, a gambling casino of the Oneida Indians of the Iroquois Nation in upstate New York, numbered playing cards morph into a serpentine wall. At the casino bar, patrons sit facing the faces of face cards rendered in fluorescent colors.

Large murals devoted to sports and leisure activities mark various break-out rooms in a Philip Morris plant near Richmond, Virginia. Each image illustrates the room's number in a memorable way.

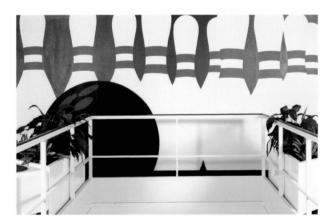

Playing with scale can embrace great and small alike...and sometimes both, side by side.

This foldout for a special millennium edition of *Forbes* magazine casts its eye from the micro to the macro.

Slivers of images range from those made by the smallest electron microscope data to the almost unimaginable dimensions of the heavens captured by radio telescopes.

The Universal Moment

In the time it takes to read this sentence, uncountable events are occurring at the atomic level. Compare these seemingly minute events to the greatest duration of all, the existence of the universe. Although the difference between the age of the universe and the passage of a photon across an atomic nucleus seems incredibly vast, both are still only mere slices within the broad spectrum of infinity.

Our own consciousness falls somewhere in the middle of this array. But the brevity of this short span deprives us of the ability to observe 100% of all occurrences. For instance, we can admire the beauty of the Appalachian Mountains, but we will never have the ability to observe their formation.

Nonetheless, mankind has made a valiant effort to chart—if never to know—all the events of our physical world. Unlike any other creature, we possess imagination, the ability to dream of this immense timescale, enabling us to transcend our brief interval on earth.

13 billion years: Age of the universe
12 billion years: Milky Way has existed
4.6 billion years: Sun has provided light to the planets
3.9 billion years: Earth has existed
3.8 billion years: Earth has sustained life
1.4 billion years: Organisms with internal cell structures have existed
750 million years: How often continents re-form
300 million years: Time necessary to create Appalachian Mountain range
208 million years: Species of birds have existed
115 million years: Span of time dinosaurs roamed earth
100 million years: How often extinction-causing meteorites collide with earth
55 million years: Length of time it takes mountain ranges to erode to sea level
10 million years: Lifetime of a star before it explodes into a supernova
3.6 million years: How long it took Hominids to evolve into Homo sapiens
100,000 years: Light travels across our galaxy
66,000 years: Length of an average ice age
24,000 years: The half-life of plutonium
10,000 years: Melting ice sheets cause 80-meter rise in ocean level
2,500 years: Average life span of a giant sequoia
248 years: Pluto circles the sun
100 years: Maximum life span of a palm tree
75 years: Halley's Comet completes one orbit
11 years: Sunspot cycle
6 years: The moon moves a foot away from the earth

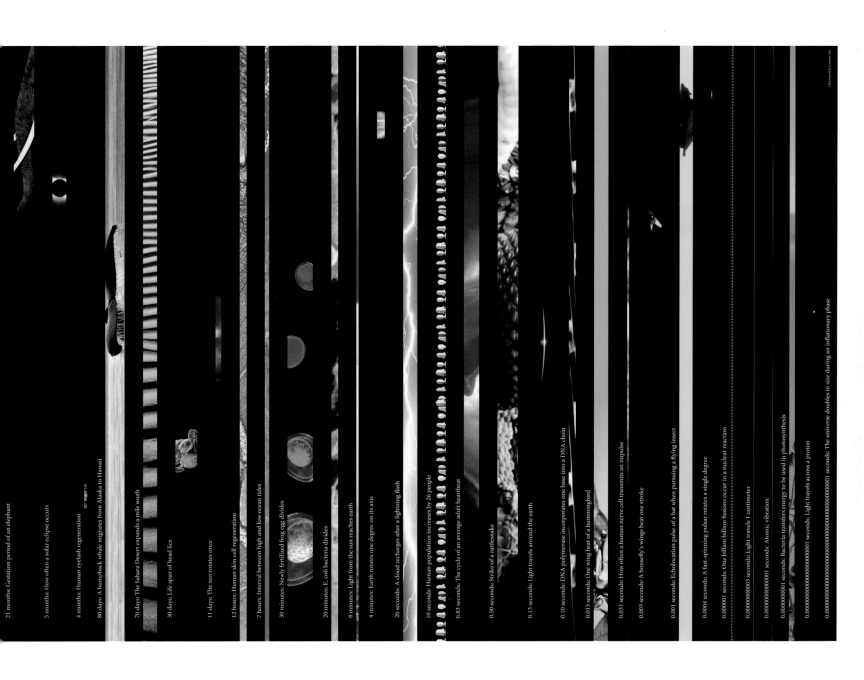

21 months: Gestation period of an elephant

5 months: How often a solar eclipse occurs

4 months: Human eyelash regeneration

80 days: A humpback whale migrates from Alaska to Hawaii

70 days: The Sahara Desert expands a mile south

30 days: Life span of head lice

11 days: The sun rotates once

12 hours: Human skin cell regeneration

7 hours: Interval between high and low ocean tides

30 minutes: Newly fertilized frog egg divides

20 minutes: E. coli bacteria divides

8 minutes: Light from the sun reaches earth

4 minutes: Earth rotates one degree on its axis

20 seconds: A cloud recharges after a lightning flash

10 seconds: Human population increases by 26 people

0.83 seconds: The cycle of an average adult heartbeat

0.50 seconds: Strike of a rattlesnake

0.13 seconds: Light travels around the earth

0.10 seconds: DNA polymerase incorporates one base into a DNA chain

0.015 seconds: One wing beat of a hummingbird

0.031 seconds: How often a human nerve cell transmits an impulse

0.003 seconds: A housefly's wings beat one stroke

0.001 seconds: Echolocation pulse of a bat when pursuing a flying insect

0.0004 seconds: A fast-spinning pulsar rotates a single degree

0.000001 seconds: One billion billion fissions occur in a nuclear reaction

0.00000000003 seconds: Light travels 1 centimeter

0.00000000000001 seconds: Atomic vibration

0.0000000001 seconds: Bacteria transfers energy to be used in photosynthesis

0.000000000000000000001 seconds: Light travels across a proton

0.00000000000000000000000000000000001 seconds: The universe doubles in size during an inflationary phase

The machine in the movie *Honey, I Shrunk the Kids* is fictional. Yet, there is a device that can indeed alter the size of objects: perspective. All visual communicators know that shifting the angle, position, or point of view makes the subject appear larger, smaller, farther away, or right in your face. Designers often change scale to exaggerate a point, to focus attention, or to make something interesting or more important.

The enormous prow of a giant oil tanker is emphasized by the relative scale of the people in the photograph on the cover of a Xerox annual report.

The outsize boots of Paul Bunyan were used as a metaphor for superhuman size and strength for an exhibit on productivity at the National Museum of American History.

a special report

XEROX 1976

The Elmer Holmes Bobst
Library and Study Center

New York University

back to that of an almost
normal floor.

Looking up a stack of railroad-
car-sized Seatrain shipping
containers makes us aware of
our own human scale, cap-
turing a perspective perpendic-
ular to the logo's directional
arrows. Without anything else
in sight to anchor us, the photograph is ambiguous about
whether we are looking up, or
looking flat along the ground.

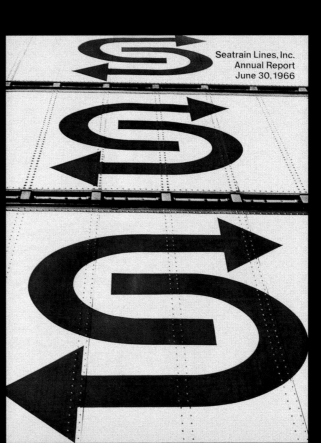

Seatrain Lines, Inc.
Annual Report
June 30, 1966

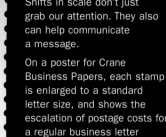

POSTAGE

1917 — 3 CENTS 3 — U.S. POSTAGE

1919 — 2 CENTS — HARDING

1932 — 3 CENTS — OLYMPIC

1958 — 4¢ — JOS. KOSSUTH—GOVERNOR OF HUNGARY, 1849 — UNITED STATES POSTAGE — OLYMPIC LIBERTY

1917-91 U.S. Postage Multiplies By Ten. • Now priced at 29¢ for a one-ounce First • Class letter, a little postage stamp is • a big deal, and a 4¢ Crane letterhead

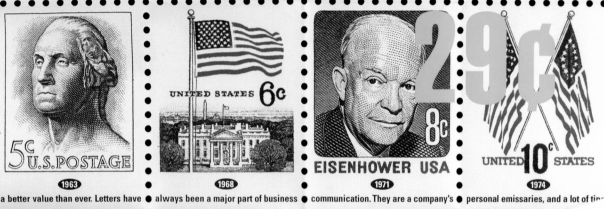

29¢

1963 — 5¢ U.S. POSTAGE (Washington)

1968 — UNITED STATES 6¢

1971 — EISENHOWER USA 8¢ — 2

1974 — UNITED 10¢ STATES

a better value than ever. Letters have • always been a major part of business • communication. They are a company's • personal emissaries, and a lot of time

CRANE

1975 — United States 13c

1978 — 15c — USA

1981 — USA 18¢

1981 — USA 20c — Truman

and money are invested in creating • and sending them. Still, your company's • letterhead is likely the only part of the • process that people see. So why buy

4¢

1985 — USA 22 — New England Neptune

1988 — USA 25 — LOVE

1991 — 29 USA

a letterhead that's less than the best? • Trust your investment to the one paper • that makes economic sense. Buy Crane.

Shifts in scale don't just grab our attention. They also can help communicate a message.

On a poster for Crane Business Papers, each stamp is enlarged to a standard letter size, and shows the escalation of postage costs for a regular business letter since 1917 compared to the still relatively small cost of a sheet of quality paper.

With a name like Best, it is hard to resist giving a little boost to the hierarchy implicit in the notion of good, better, best. For three-dimensional applications, the letters diminish in width as they grow in height, getting progressively thinner as they get larger. The innovative store architecture developed by the firm Site integrated the logo into the building itself.

BEST

For the U.S. pavilion at the Osaka World's Fair in 1970, artists were paired with technology companies to create unique, creative works of art. Claes Oldenburg has always experimented effectively with scale in his sculpture, and his huge ice bag is no exception. For a mostly Japanese audience, of course, it wasn't just the scale but the foreign object itself that drew attention.

Cleaning the buildings of Rockefeller Center is a monumental task, not to be undertaken lightly (or by anyone who doesn't do windows). A 35-foot-high inflated figure announces that the site's new owner is about to take on the job. The figure's extraordinary size seems to shrink the building by comparison, making a daunting task seem a bit less formidable.

Taking artistic license
Erasing the line between art and design

Painter or illustrator? Copywriter or author? Artist or designer? The distinctions are familiar. But are they useful? When designers act as problem-solvers and communicators, when they focus on order and clarity and content, their destination may indeed differ from that of the artist. But travelers with different destinations frequently share the same highway. They may even drive the same cars. Distinctions can prove elusive.

Design can create an occasion for art, an opportunity for art. It may entail a search for ways to make the ordinary extraordinary, to trigger a stimulating experience, or simply to take a new look at a familiar task. In every field, much is made of those who "push the envelope." Art often means discarding the envelope.

Assemblage and collage are all about putting good stuff together to make something new and delicious. And as in cooking, the dish is tastier when assembled from top-quality ingredients.

A Museum of Modern Art book on the subject uses 19th-century type to spell out "Assemblage."

The front and back covers of the very first issue of the *AIGA Journal*, published in 1965, feature a construction of presstype letters that create a dense carpet of illegible typographic forms and counter forms.

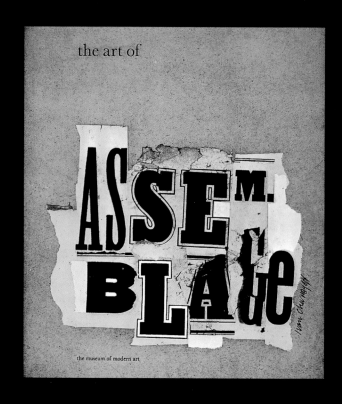

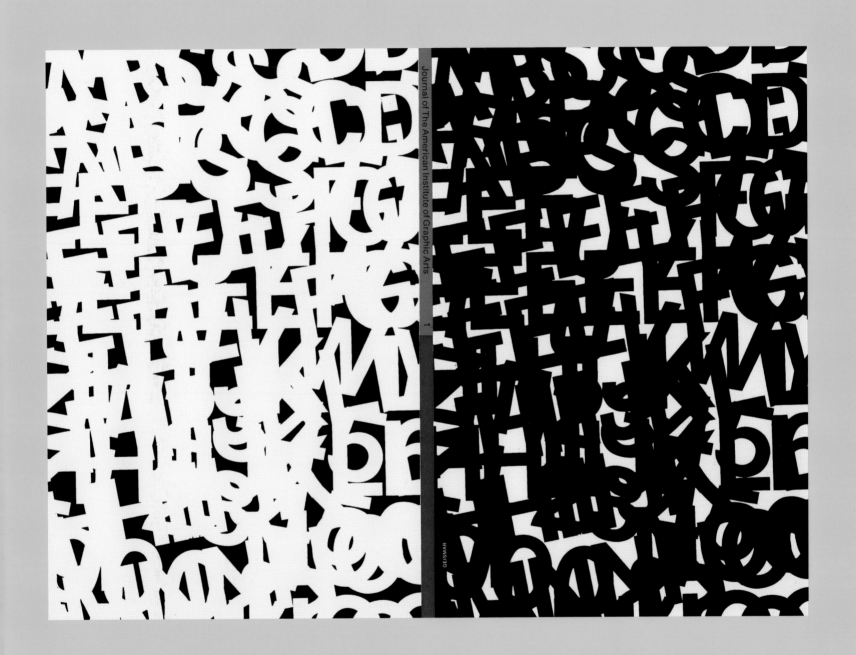

Journal of The American Institute of Graphic Arts

1

GEISMAR

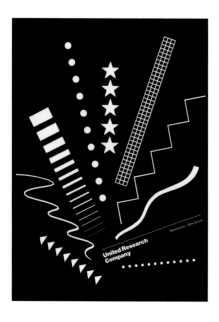

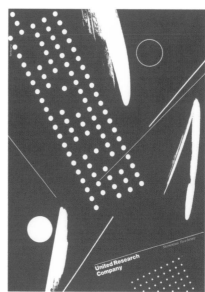

Abstract and geometric shapes and lines, unencumbered by the direct associations that come with recognizable objects, lend themselves to expressions of motion and emotion. Abstract interpretations of dance in these donor-supported ads for New York City Ballet's annual program stand out effectively from the dance photography that more typically adorns such publications.

Sometimes, it's possible to combine two visual vocabularies seamlessly, leaving the impression that the two languages actually belong together. This takes artistic license to a new height. One season's promotion for the Jacob's Pillow Dance Festival experimented with combining the markings of abstract expressionist action painting with a high-contrast, photograph. The fused image creates a new way to accomplish the difficult task of capturing the action of dance.

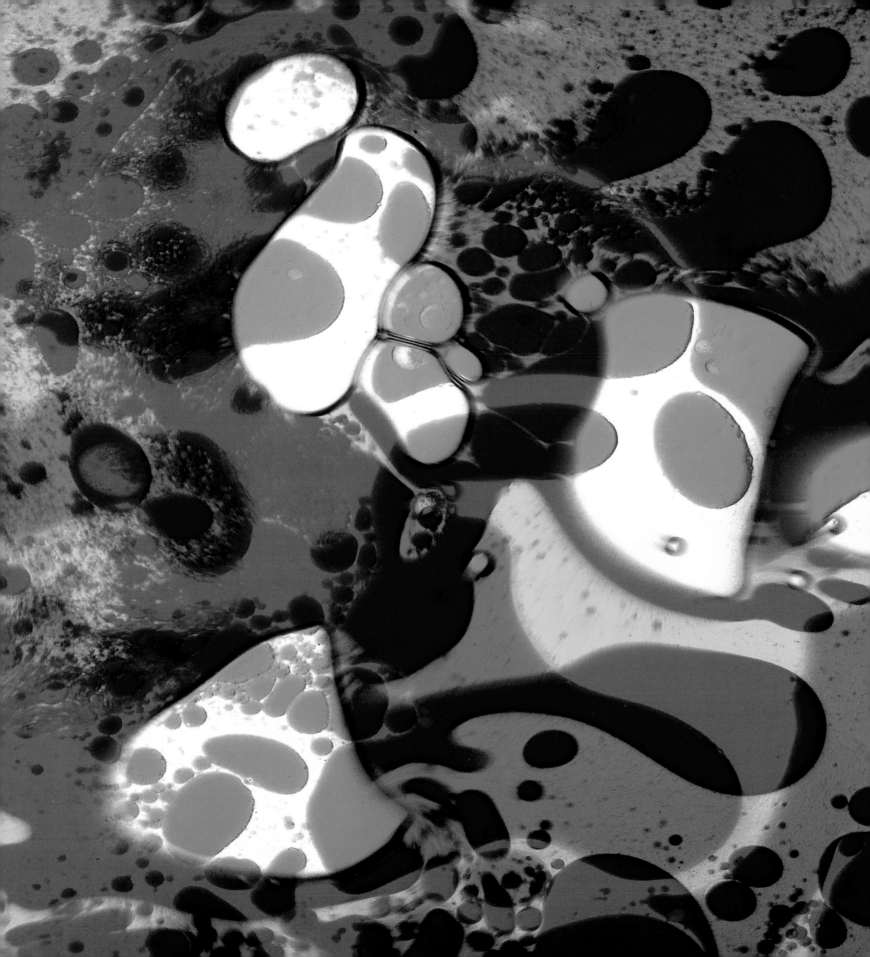

Designers can often recognize inherent artistic qualities in the most mundane materials.

An image capturing the forms and colors of overlapping, liquid printing inks is used for the cover of a publication on lithographic inks, one in a series of booklets for Monadnock Papers.

The cover of a promotional sketchbook features a blind embossing of a collage made from actual recycled cotton material, such as clippings from T-shirts and blankets used in the process of making Crane's 100% cotton papers.

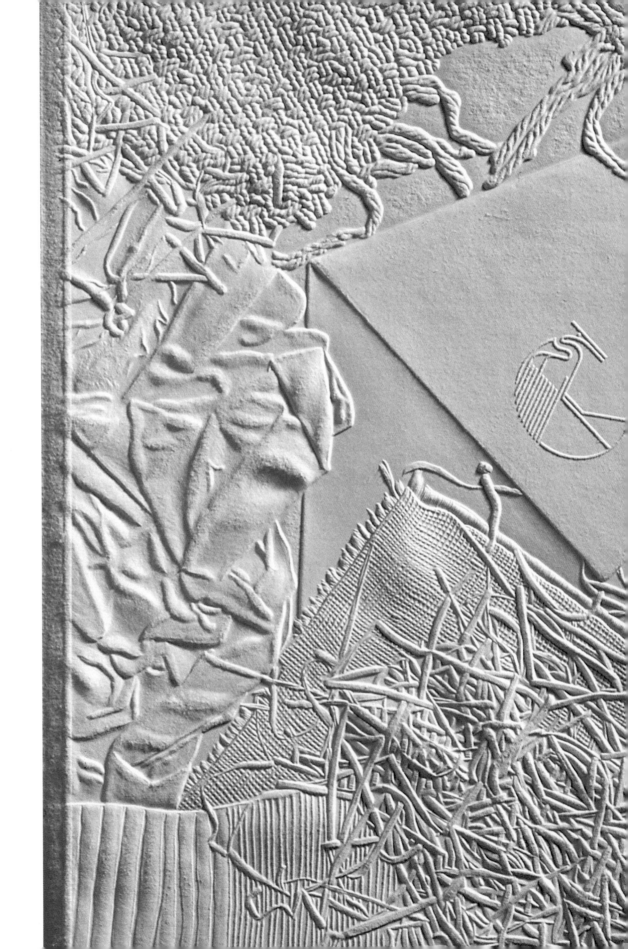

Collage is the process of gathering, seeing, and finding connections to create an image. The license taken is in asking the viewer to accept the pieces and their new meaning as a single expression, despite its many, sometimes eclectic, components. If the rules have been established clearly enough, the result is a piece of art. Or maybe design. Does it really matter which?

For the cover of a catalog of summer sessions in the arts at UCLA, a still life was created from an actual pencil, cut and torn paper, pieces of origami paper, inked brushstrokes, and grease pencil scrawlings. The old-fashioned idea of a still life and the more modern assemblage approach at once suggests both tradition and modernity.

For a poster for fellowships at the American Academy in Rome, a collage was created from past academy catalogs and invitations as a reminder of the institution's accomplishments and activities. An overrun of the poster was cut up to make menu covers for the annual dinner—in essence, fragments of fragments.

Pieces of posters and print promotions come together in a collage for the cover of the magazine *Idea* where the name of the magazine reads clearly.

The logotype for the printing firm named "Colorcraft" is an assembly of colors and letters. Graphic designers, art directors, museum staff, and others in the arts community are the primary audience, a savvy target group that allows for greater artistic license with little risk of misunderstanding.

Every circus needs its ring-master. When you're trying to group a cavalcade of related but diverse elements, a common denominator—a unifying technique, material, or framework—can help to bind the discrete elements and expressions into a coherent whole.

A poster for the AIGA's New York chapter announces various upcoming events and speakers. Recognizable fragments, symbols and icons form a collage that implies windows and frames. The reader is looking through a series of spaces to catch a glimpse of what is to come.

The poster was also printed on heavy stock and cut into equal-size postcards. The randomly fragmented cards were then used to announce individual events, with the appropriate information printed on the back.

For the television series *Pride of Place: Building the American Dream*, a poster depicts a single building made from a wide variety of familiar architectural styles, all melded into one Escher-like edifice. The image became an icon for the show in advertising and related publishing ventures.

Mobil

Working with local artisans lets designers take advantage of special talents and a regional heritage. It is a way of involving others in the design process and instilling a sense of local pride and forming tangible community ties.

This approach brings a distinctive sensibility and flavor to pieces created for the public areas of a large North Carolina manufacturing plant.

Fifty-four women and one man were commissioned to craft one-foot square appliqués in the geometric designs of classic quilts, using cotton fabrics in a prescribed palette of colors. The quilters, all from North Carolina, got together for a quilting bee. The result is the largest hanging quilt in the world, as far as we know.

In another area of the plant, a striped wall, was created from fabric woven on small hand looms by local weavers.

Three cheers for captive audiences. They make it much easier to take artistic liberties. They embolden the creative urge by reducing fear of failure (or at least, the immediate consequences of failure).

The Mobil logotype, with its red "o" and the company's Pegasus symbol, are, of course, familiar symbols to Mobil employees. Cut into squares of equal size and appliquéd together, they become artistic variations on the firm's major identity elements—transformed from corporate images into decorative additions for stairwells at the company's U.K. headquarters in Swindon, outside London.

A visual/verbal interpretation of the theme "Wishful Thinking" was prepared for a design magazine. The two words of the theme have been taken apart, making them "wish", "full", "thin" and "king", and then illustrated in two different artistic ways.

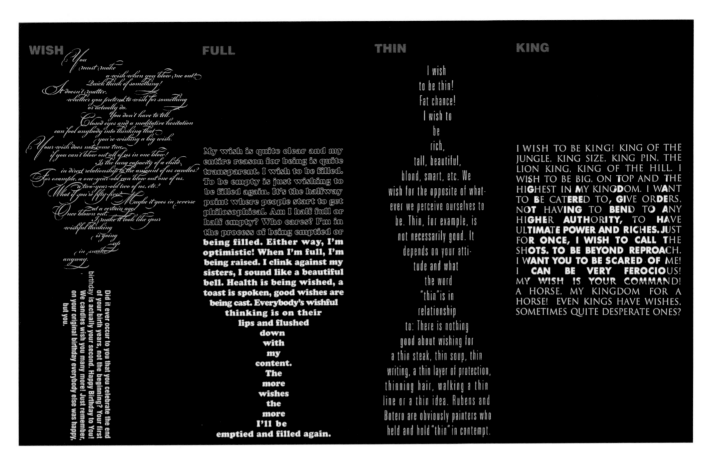

WISH

You must make a wish when you blow one out! Quick think of something! It doesn't matter, whether you pretend to wish for something or actually do. You don't have to tell. Closed eyes and a meditative hesitation can fool anybody into thinking that you're wishing a big wish. Your wish does not come true if you can't blow out all of us in one blow! Is the lung capacity of a child in direct relationship to the amount of us candles? For example, a one-year-old can blow out one of us, a two-year-old two of us, etc.? What if you're fifty-five? Maybe it goes in reverse. Once blown out at a certain age? I make it look like your wistful thinking is going up in smoke anyway.

Did it ever occur to you that you celebrate the end of your birth years, not the beginning? Your first birthday is actually your second. Happy Birthday to You! We candles wish you many more! Just remember, on your original birthday everybody else was happy, but you.

FULL

My wish is quite clear and my entire reason for being is quite transparent. I wish to be filled. To be empty is just wishing to be filled again. It's the halfway point where people start to get philosophical. Am I half full or half empty? Who cares? I'm in the process of being emptied or being filled. Either way, I'm optimistic! When I'm full, I'm being raised. I clink against my sisters, I sound like a beautiful bell. Health is being wished, a toast is spoken, good wishes are being cast. Everybody's wishful thinking is on their lips and flushed down with my content. The more wishes the more I'll be emptied and filled again.

THIN

I wish to be thin! Fat chance! I wish to be rich, tall, beautiful, blond, smart, etc. We wish for the opposite of whatever we perceive ourselves to be. Thin, for example, is not necessarily good. It depends on your attitude and what the word "thin" is in relationship to: There is nothing good about wishing for a thin steak, thin soup, thin writing, a thin layer of protection, thinning hair, walking a thin line or a thin idea. Rubens and Botero are obviously painters who held and hold "thin" in contempt.

KING

I WISH TO BE KING! KING OF THE JUNGLE. KING SIZE. KING PIN. THE LION KING. KING OF THE HILL. I WISH TO BE BIG, ON TOP AND THE HIGHEST IN MY KINGDOM. I WANT TO BE CATERED TO, GIVE ORDERS, NOT HAVING TO BEND TO ANY HIGHER AUTHORITY, TO HAVE ULTIMATE POWER AND RICHES. JUST FOR ONCE, I WISH TO CALL THE SHOTS. TO BE BEYOND REPROACH. I WANT YOU TO BE SCARED OF ME! I CAN BE VERY FEROCIOUS! MY WISH IS YOUR COMMAND! A HORSE, MY KINGDOM FOR A HORSE! EVEN KINGS HAVE WISHES, SOMETIMES QUITE DESPERATE ONES?

Utility often is the starting point for design. But it need not be the stopping point. Taking artistic license often means going beyond the utilitarian.

A theme of circles, squares, and triangles derives from the shapes and footprint of a Philip Morris plant in Virginia. In a pool outside the cafeteria and executive offices, the design motif evolved into cubes, tetrahedrons, and cylindrical shapes. Their 30-foot height is seemingly doubled by reflection in the pool.

The same geometric themes continue on the main interior wall of the cafeteria. There, hidden neon tubing reflects the strong colors painted on the back of raised circular, square, and triangular shapes.

A square grid of 49 steel posts, painted NYPD blue, marks the entrance to the 49th police precinct in the Bronx.

Art and technology joined forces at the U.S. pavilion at Expo'70 in Osaka, Japan. A maze of laser beams shoots across and bounces off the mirrored surfaces of a tunnel-like space through which visitors walk.

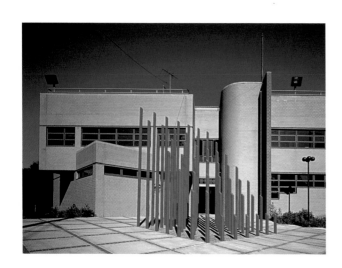

In the interior of a savings bank, taking liberties with the treatment of walls and other surfaces, transforms the space.

What looks at first like a pile of rocks in the reception area of Gemini Consulting's training center is in fact a novel form of seating. Carved and spray-painted pieces of foam serve as movable "chairs" for trainees. Trainees simply claim a rock and sit on it wherever and whenever needed. After the session, the rocks are returned to the pile.

Repeating, repeating
Creating more than the sum of its parts

Any single element—be it a letterform, a toy, a common household item, or an abstract shape—takes on a completely different form when multiplied and repeated. What seems uninteresting by itself looks intriguing as a repeated image, whether the items are arranged by design or at random.

The image of a music stand seems at first a mundane choice for an annual report cover of an instrument manufacturer. But multiplied, the stands make beautiful music together.

In another piece, the rhythmic patterns of keys, levers, and caps of wind instruments look almost like sheet music notations. The dense pattern of shapes echoes the brilliant, quick, and silvery sound of these exquisite instruments.

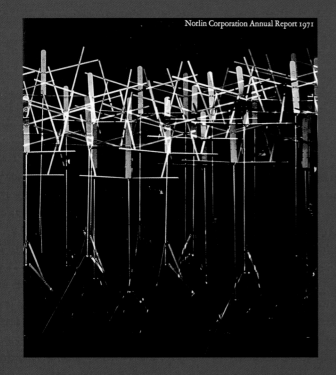

Norlin Corporation Annual Report 1971

Why did Edgar Allan Poe write about "the tintinnabulation that so musically wells/From the bells, bells, bells, bells/Bells, bells, bells"? Wouldn't one or two bells have sufficed?

Everybody knows that there's safety in numbers. Like Poe, designers know that there is also interest and meaning in saying things more then once. Repeating an image—or a family of related images—transforms a lonely individual into something greater. Just as a single living cell takes on new vitality, purpose, and potential when joined with others to form some larger organism, so individual items, replicated and recombined, become part of a greater whole.

Repetition can create a sense of energy and mobility. It can suggest relationships and hierarchies, charging the mundane with new meaning.

Less is not always more. "Sometimes more is not nearly enough," as a flamboyant friend used to say.

Ten thousand Christmas balls cover a giant ribbon to celebrate the 1959 holiday season in the lobby of Pepsi-Cola's headquarters on Park Avenue in New York. The balls merge their individuality, becoming like pixels in a digital picture (even in that pre-digital year). Two clichés—tree ornaments and ribbons—join forces to make a new and original image.

For a holiday window display, stacked boxes covered with Pepsi bottle caps lend texture, novelty, and a specific corporate imprint to commonplace holiday objects.

A single flower versus a bouquet, a single hair versus a head of it, completely changes the perception of each item. A single matchstick looks like a piece of cardboard with a red tip. In a matchbook, it looks like one in a row of soldiers ready to strike.

The black sheep is a symbol created for the Old Chatham Sheepherding Company's line of sheep cheeses. The ovine logo appears on packaging, labels, signs, trucks, advertising, and promotional material. Matchbooks for the Old Chatham Sheepherding Company Inn are herded together.

In a mural at the Genoa Aquarium, repetition of fish heads and tails and fins, scales and tentacles reflects the ever-changing, constantly-in-motion life of the ocean.

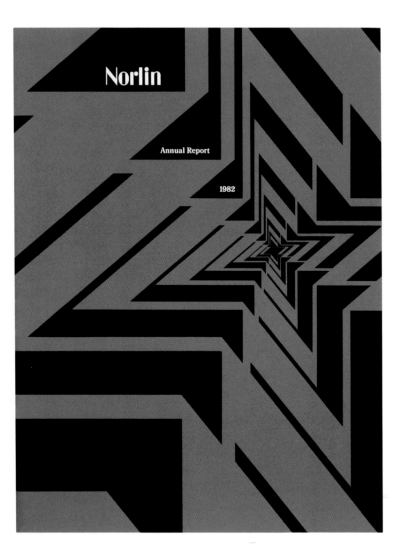

Repetition is the simplest way to create a pattern.

In wrapping for Xerox photocopier papers, or gift wrap for Brentano's bookstore, words, logos, and letterforms blend together to form an attractive pattern.

The Norlin logo itself is made up of four repeated and rotated N's, creating a star-like inner shape. Repeated, reduced, and stepped back, the pattern creates the illusion of three-dimensional space.

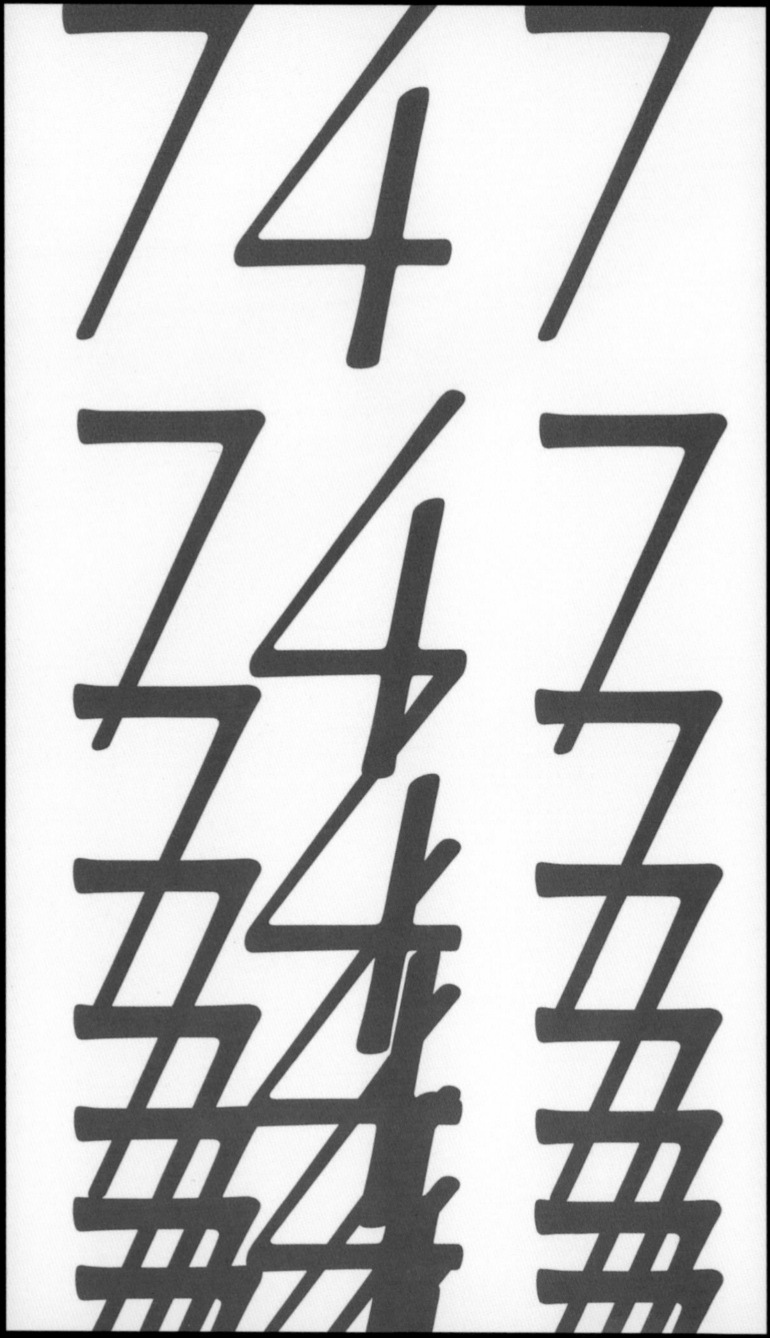
747

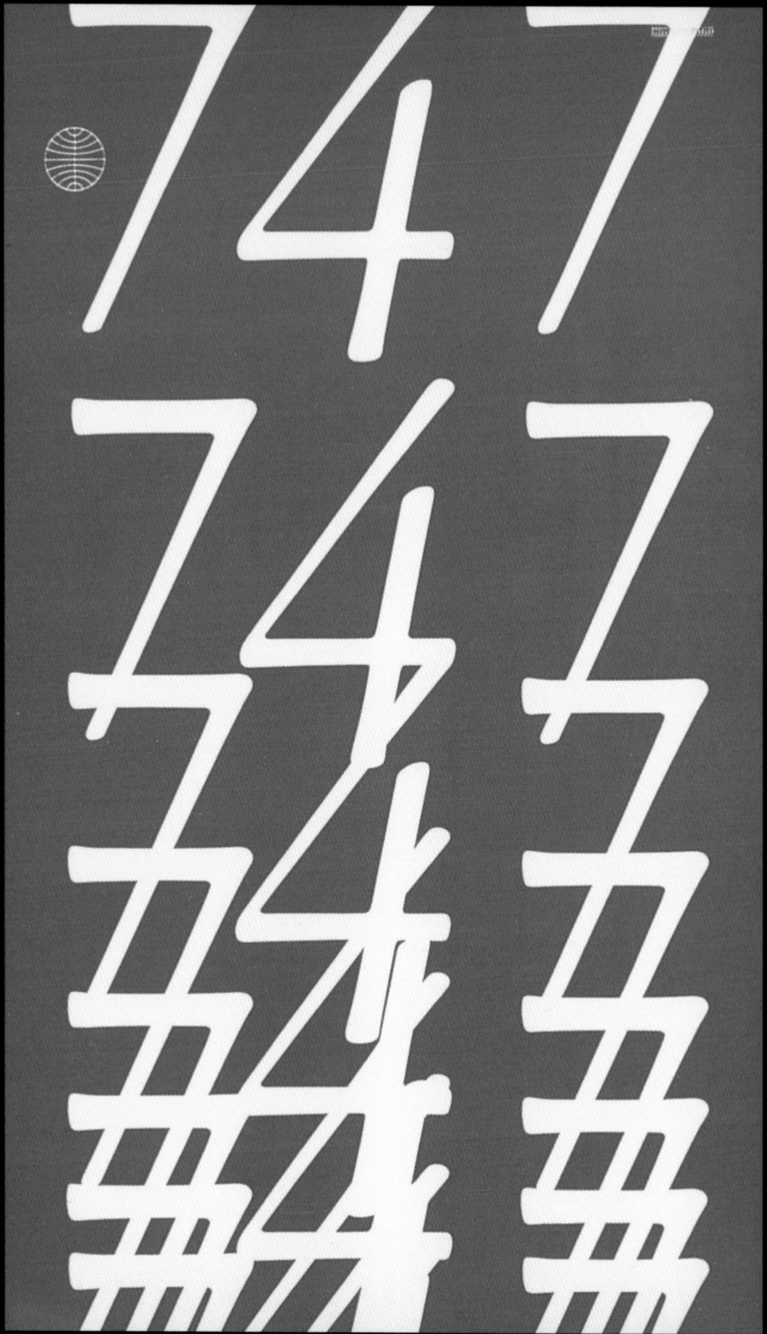
747

Stack, shift, step, and repeat. Progressions and gradations are all techniques of creating sequences and patterns, of playing with positive and negative spaces to create new shapes.

On Pan Am's inaugural flight of the Boeing 747, from New York to Paris, commemorative menus in the first-class cabin celebrated the event. Through typographic repetition and careful spacing, the 747 takes off and soars.

Packaging for personal packets of moist towelettes is designed so that the product name wraps around the edges of the box. This meant that it would in fact "wash up" onto the package above or below when stacked in a drugstore or supermarket.

How can you use repetition without repeating yourself?

The May Department Stores logotype and color scheme were, for many years, the primary graphic expressions on its annual report covers. The challenge was to reinvent the concept anew each year while at the same time finding a way to visually reflect the layout inside the report.

A simple pattern of white diamonds suggests snow, and establishes a design for all May Department Store Company's holiday packaging. This motif reappeared throughout the stores for many years on festive displays, banners, boxes, and shopping bags.

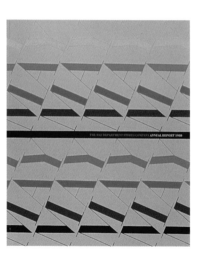

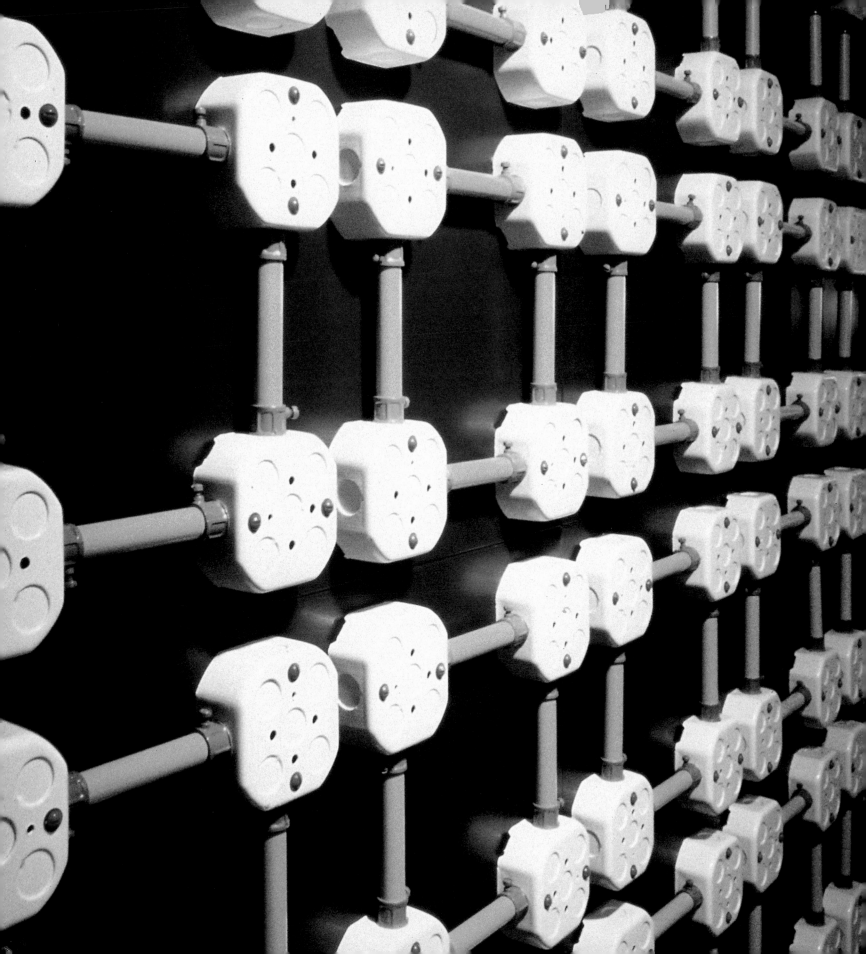

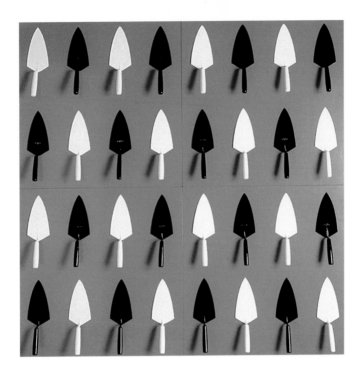

Repetition can act like an intoxicating visual drug. It draws you into its detail and, at the same time, makes you dizzy with its seemingly never ending and expanding rhythms.

Bouygues is the largest construction company in France, specializing in heavy construction—bridges, highways, and other projects that aren't usually featured on the Do-It-Yourself Channel. The company offices outside Paris were decorated with large wall pieces fashioned from the tools and supplies of the construction trade, collected, painted, and repeated in patterns. Junction boxes, trowels, bolts, spanners, wrenches, and the like appear on five floors of the firm's headquarters.

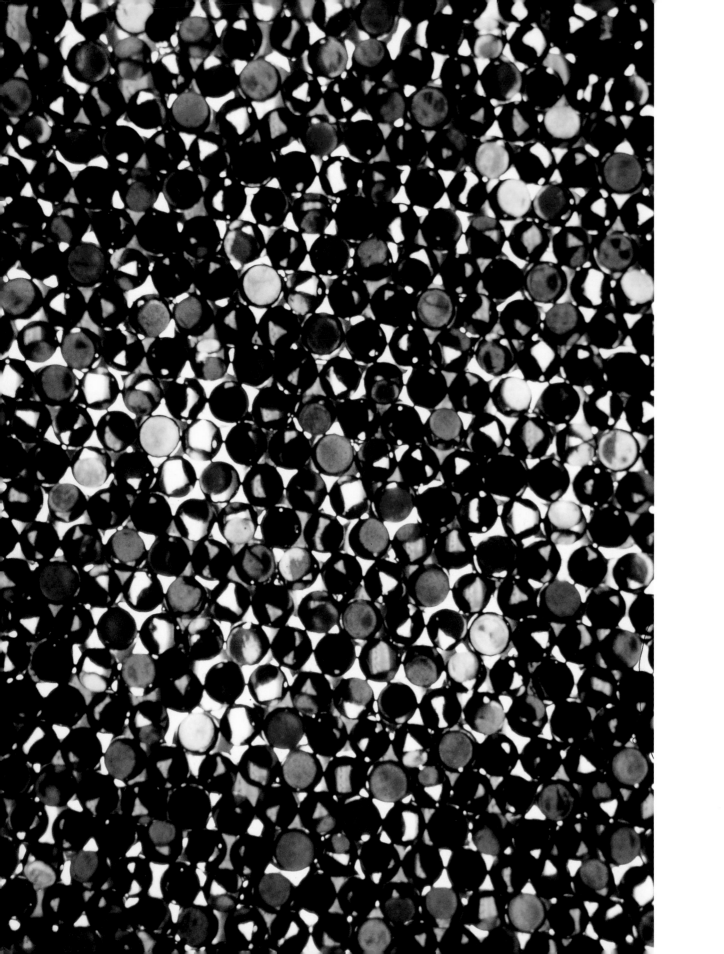

A massing of related objects or forms, combined with light and movement, can suggest natural effects.

At the New England Aquarium in Boston, light refracted through a mass of aquarium marbles, sandwiched between large sheets of glass, evokes the ever-changing quality of water as the visitor passes by.

On the ceiling of the Tennessee Aquarium, continually changing colored light, passing through flexible light-conducting tubes, gives the sense of the restless surface of the ocean.

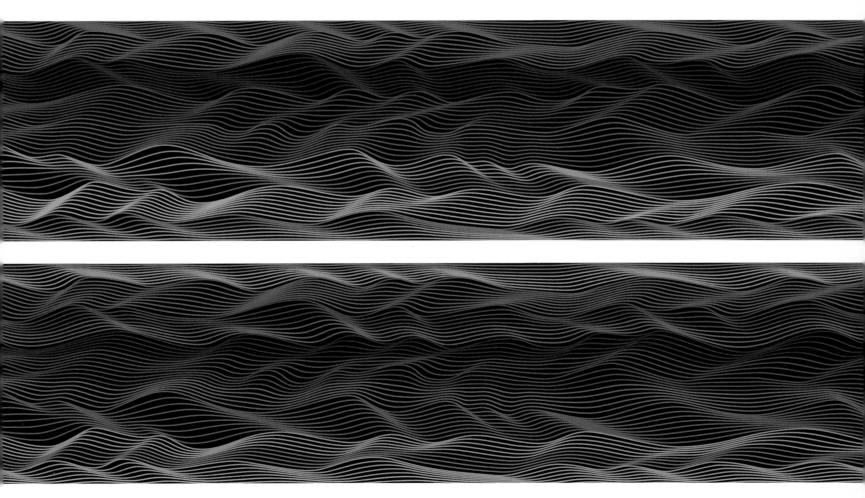

Realizing ideas
Sparking instant understanding

...and send us your best entries. The 59th Annual Exhibition of The Art Directors Club of New York.

...BEST OF TRAFFIC...

Being "on top of the world" does not mean that, like Edmund Hillary or Tenzing Norgay, you're peering down from Everest. Calling someone "yellow" is not a diagnosis of jaundice. Saying that someone is "hard as nails" is not a license to hit them on the head. In language, we readily juggle the physical and the figurative to get a point across.

Design can do likewise, playing with metaphors and forms to forge evocative, intriguing links. Design can give established ideas new energy, taking familiar ideas and imagery into unfamiliar territory by using common-place phrases or images as a starting point from which to explore and manipulate concepts, to realize ideas.

We've all heard that actions speak louder than words. This design counts on that. The sign says "Stop", but the action implied by the tire tracks shows that someone didn't. So this call for entries for the New York Art Directors Club suggests that readers too should ignore the command. The unspoken message is that the best advertising work breaks molds, ignores expectations, and challenges rules.

The poster for an exhibition at the Museum of Contemporary Art in Los Angeles uses the vernacular of Detroit to evoke the personality of an automobile. For the exhibition poster, one-piece cast metal lettering was made, then photographed against the glossy surface of an automobile. This is not so much a case of action speaking louder than words as *materials* speaking louder than words.

Automobile
and
Culture

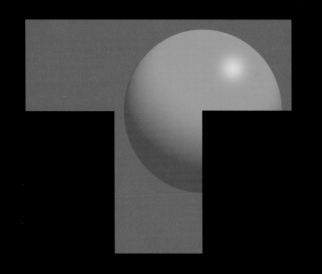

An effective identity does not require a single symbolic image. A broad idea, or a family of related images, can also forge a recognizable persona. Like a composer, the designer establishes a theme, then revels in variations on that theme. This approach works well for television, where sequential or animated images are possible.

The concept for Telemundo, a Hispanic-language television network, is that the letter "T" forms a window onto the world. "Tele" is an abbreviation for "television" and "mundo" is the Spanish word for "world." Once established, this idea becomes a starting point for variations, such as replacing the globe inside the "T" with other circular objects— balloons, flowers, or balls, perhaps—to announce individual programs. The logo with the soccer ball became the identity for all World Soccer Cup broadcasting. Telemundo's identity is first established with a simple idea...then extended with playful twists.

For WGBH, the public television station in Boston, the essential idea was to make the channel number in a three-dimensional form. Design applications then brought the symbol to life by treating it as a character, and animating it in many ways. After adopting this concept in 1974, the WGBH staff developed specific program identities that played off it, such as a cake in the form of a "2" for Julia Child's cooking show, and a timber construction "2" for the program *About the House*.

WGBH also developed a "2-mobile," built over the chassis of a Volkswagen and used to tour Massachusetts, raising funds for the non-profit public television station. The public could "keep WGBH running" by putting contributions in a slot in the back of the vehicle.

About the House

The Way It Was

Leonardo

Channel 2-Mobile
Public Television in Boston

WGBH·2

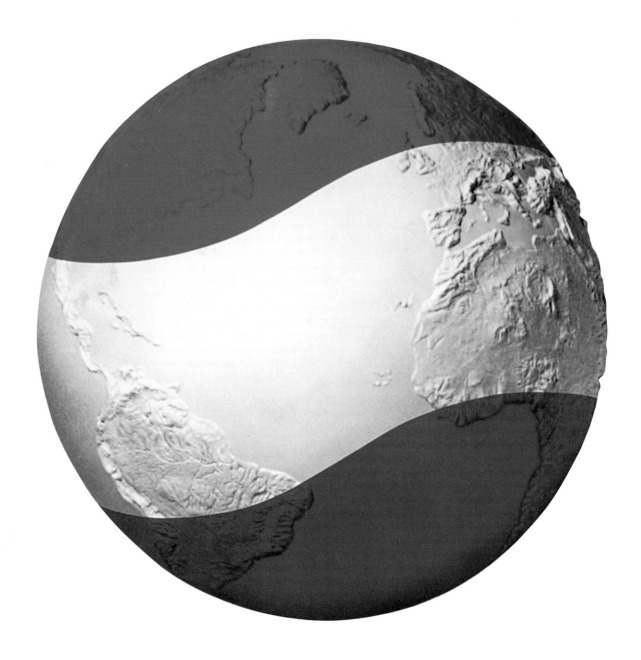

At times, designers can capitalize on an instantly recognized element of a company's product, making it serve as a visual identifier for the company.

The Pepsi-Cola bottle cap, with its distinctive red, white, and blue wave forms, is a part of the American landscape. Everyone recognizes it. And in design, such instant recognition is a prized asset, not to be squandered lightly.

One Pepsi annual report cover uses the wave forms alone, superimposed on a topographic globe. Another cover uses a bottle cap as a stand-in for a globe, clearly implying the international scope of the company.

The theme of the month for Pepsi-Cola's in-house magazine could easily have been mired in cliché. Visually manipulating the components of this ubiquitous product—bottle caps, cartons, bottles, cases, and six-packs—made the familiar fun and appropriate for an in-house audience.

The themes shown are March winds, Easter baskets, April showers, May flowers, June bride, July sport, summer vacation, August fishing, autumn harvest, October football, Thanksgiving, and Christmas.

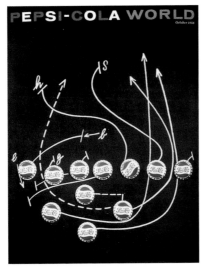

SOUND CONTROL

You can express ideas directly. Or you can convey them *indirectly,* by association.

The taped mouth of a young girl suggests sound control, the theme of an issue of *Architectural and Engineering News.*

A single cinder block done up as a building appears on the cover of an issue devoted to block construction.

Other tools of the architectural profession also lend themselves to visual manipulation. Drafting triangles form a Christmas star for a holiday greeting from the architectural office of Edward Larrabee Barnes. The erasing shield, with its ornamental-looking shapes, lends itself to reinterpretation as a Christmas greeting for the Edgewood Furniture Company, its functional shapes gaining seasonal verve as holiday ornaments.

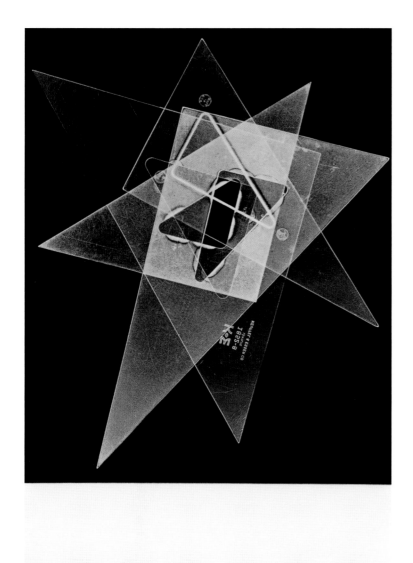

MERRY CHRISTMAS AND HAPPY NEW YEAR / EDWARD L. BARNES AND ASSOCIATES

⚝ **EDGEWOOD**   a collection conceived in architectural terms for executive and public spaces by William Armbruster

Write for our new catalogue and illustrated price list. Factory-showroom: 334 E. 75th St., N.Y.

HERMAN WOUK'S
WAR
AND
REMEMBRANCE

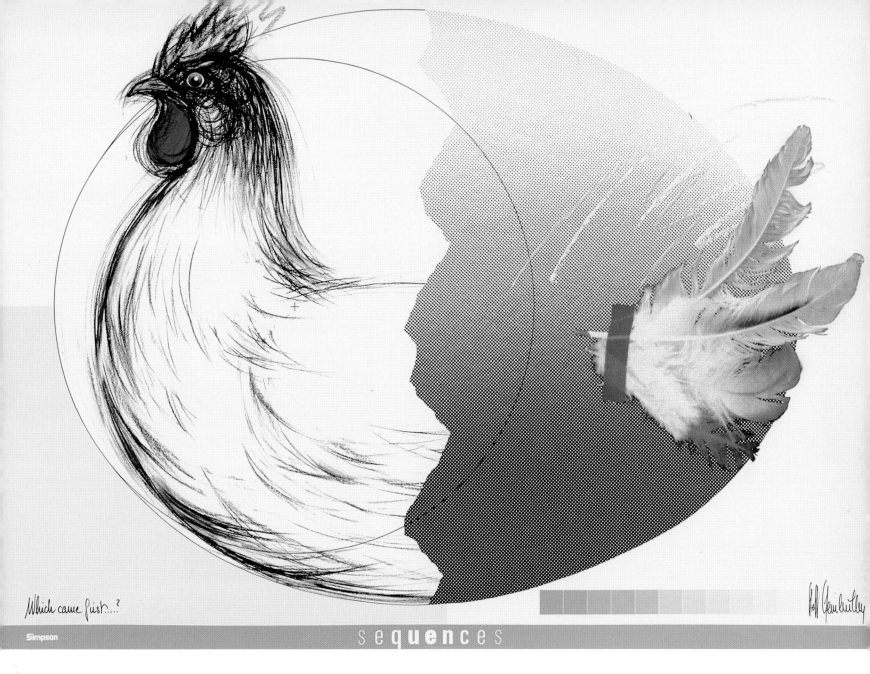

Which came first....?

Simpson

se**qu**en**c**es

Metaphors are a powerful shorthand for ideas. Combining them can create new images that trumpet bold messages.

An advertising image for a television version of a novel puts a rose on a stem of barbed wire with its thorns of war.

Which came first, the chicken or the egg…or the design idea of combining them? The egg melds with the chicken to become a single image for a paper company poster, capitalizing on a timeless conundrum to interpret the theme of "sequences".

The Fall and Rise of Tinicum Marsh 1900's

The Dawn of Industry 1800's

Settling the New World 1643-1800

Original People   Lenape

Designers and artists excel at creating their own reality. But sometimes, the real reality is more effective. When conveying ideas in three-dimensional form, as in nature-related exhibits, the ideas can be made memorable by using the real stuff.

For a visitor center at the Tinicum Marsh outside of Philadelphia, the design solution recognizes that much of the most interesting life unfolds below ground. To convey this, a 100-foot-long cross-section of marsh enables the visitor to see the abundant and often over-looked life hidden beneath the surface of the actual habitat.

At the World of Birds at the Bronx Zoo, displays of live creatures surround a central room where visitors are warned of the extinction and endangerment of many bird species. One hundred tombstone-like stone markers frame the surrounding walls, each engraved with the image and name of an already extinct group. These in turn surround a series of inter-active stories about specific endangered species, what threatens them, and what can be done about it.

Guiding the way
Pinpointing destinations with visual prompts

Consider the arrow. That humble symbol is so familiar as a visual signpost that we hardly pause to think of it as graphic design. Its simplicity and utility perfectly illustrate the power of graphics to keep us on the straight and narrow—or to help us navigate the broad and winding. Design is about developing effective symbols that slice through the visual clutter, about coining a vocabulary of shapes or colors that help us navigate the world around us.

Some of the symbols—like the arrow—in the designer's toolbox are ubiquitous and universal.

At other times, the designer must come up with new symbols. Then, the goal is to devise new icons or wayfinding systems that do their work so effectively and naturally that they seem as familiar and intuitive as an arrow.

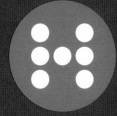

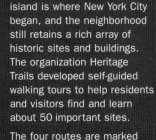

The lower tip of Manhattan island is where New York City began, and the neighborhood still retains a rich array of historic sites and buildings. The organization Heritage Trails developed self-guided walking tours to help residents and visitors find and learn about 50 important sites.

The four routes are marked with color-coded dots affixed to the sidewalk. A 40-page illustrated guidebook combines annotated maps with photographs and anecdotes about each site. Freestanding kiosks at key locations provide a more detailed history.

HERITAGE · TRAILS · NEW · YORK

Downtown at your feet!

© 1995 Heritage Trails NY, Inc.
Designed by VanDam, Inc.
All rights reserved

1/4 miles
0.4 kms

★ Heritage Trails Hub
& Visitor Information Center
Federal Hall, 26 Wall St
For more information call:
Heritage Trails New York
212-767-0637

Design elements can suggest movement and direction as well as generate delight in public places.

At a bustling New York City subway transfer concourse, bold forms and color help to guide passengers at major decision points. Directions are big, friendly, and clear. Large graffiti-proof wall panels echo the circular motif.

The lobby of the IBM building in midtown Manhattan has dark granite walls and mirror-finished ceilings. To serve as elevator indicators, a ladder of light bars, echoing the IBM logo, is cut into the granite above each of the 16 elevators. As the cars ascend and descend, the light bars illuminate, indicating the elevator cab's location and its direction of travel. The design combines entertainment and information, and what might otherwise be a static space becomes lively, animated, and informative.

19-21

There are few things more frustrating than getting lost... particularly when you have dutifully been following directions. In a large city, clarifying the twists and turns and eccentricities of a complex transit system is a monumental task.

In the mid-1960s, Boston's famed MTA expanded to include both subway and surface transportation throughout the metropolitan region. As part of the expansion, a new way-finding system introduced the simple initial T in a circle as the system identifier, since so many relevant words begin with that initial. The various lines were renamed for colors rather than for the names of their final stops, which were in constant flux as the system expanded.

A simplified, diagrammatic map reflects the color-coding of the lines, which is consistently used on all signs.

Large, clear wall maps of the surrounding neighborhood, integrated into the architects' station design, guide exiting passengers.

T:
Transportation
Transit
Train
Track
Tunnel
Tube
Ticket
Travel
Timetable
Token
Toll
Trip
Trolley

The pervasive arrow points the way again and again, guiding real or imagined traffic.

At the Temporary Contemporary museum in Los Angeles, the visual language of highway signs and arrows guide people through the one-way traffic flow of the museum's inaugural exhibition, "Automobile and Culture." The design uses the vocabulary of the road to steer visitors as they explore the aesthetic of the road.

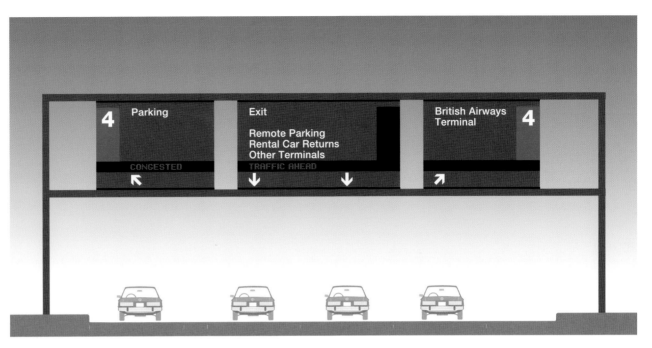

A concept for using state-of-the-art electronics and clear graphics on signs above the roadways leading into and around New York City's John F. Kennedy Airport to guide traffic at this busy place.

In a dense city like New York, parking garages more often than not are underground caverns that drivers find frightening to navigate. At one midtown site, bold colors, graphics, and lighting direct drivers dramatically and clearly to the below-ground parking levels.

Symbol Signs

How do you establish a common language among people who may not *speak* a common language? Pictures transcend borders. When limited to understandable messages, and used consistently, pictograms can effectively point travelers and tourists in the right direction, especially those who have limited understanding of the local language.

A set of pictograms developed in the 1960s for the National Park Service identifies various wayside features within the nations' parks. Intended for use along roadways and trails, the program of replacing words with bold symbols lets the signs remain small and discreet. Even when clustered together, the pictograms clearly indicate the amenities available, helping park visitors choose what they want to do.

In the 1970s, we chaired a committee of designers under the auspices of the American Institute of Graphic Arts to develop an extensive system of pictograms for the U.S. Department of Transportation. Called *Symbol Signs*, they became the U.S. standard for airports, train stations, and other transit facilities. To encourage wide-spread adoption, the symbols were offered free of charge to any qualified users. The Symbol Sign system has been the subject of exhibitions and a series of publications, and has subsequently become something of a worldwide standard.

Usually, guiding the way requires the designer to emphasize clear, concise, unencumbered graphics, especially in public facilities. But in more restricted situations, where there is a captive or constant audience, more imaginative and subtle means can enliven signposts for even the most mundane activities.

In the employee kitchen areas of Gemini Consulting, lunchtime trash is segregated into three bins so that food will be separated from cans and paperboard, which are recycled. Framed collages of actual and re-created materials, hung above the appropriate openings in the kitchen counter, tell employees what goes where.

In another kitchen, small sculptures, such as the bag with falling French fries, play the same role.

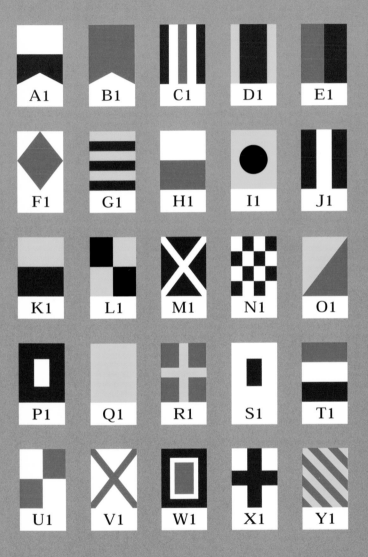

Way-finding systems can take many forms.

The Port Authority of New York and New Jersey found that passengers disembarking from large cruise ships were having difficulty locating their luggage in the 1,000-foot-long baggage halls. A system of bold hanging banners and matching luggage tags using the very graphic nautical semaphore signals alphabet helped relieve the problem.

At the observatory atop the John Hancock building in Boston, "tubescopes" clearly isolate views of buildings and sites that are of particular interest. Overhead transparencies amplify the view, providing close-up images and historically relevant facts.

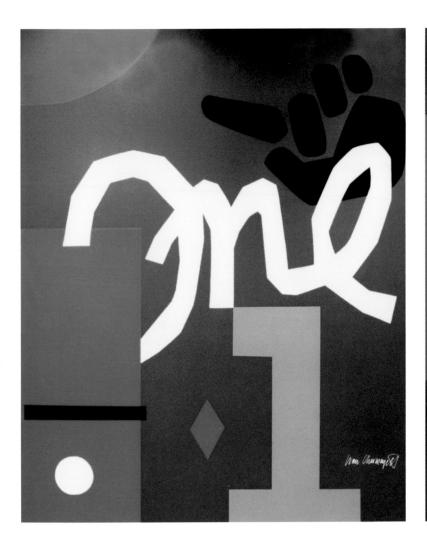

A sign does not have to be a rectangle with text. Nor must signs be thought of as a necessary evil, cluttering up the view. Instead, they can take inventive, unusual forms. They can be as intriguing as their surroundings; notable additions to the landscapes they occupy.

At a duplex movie theater, two large paintings that point patrons to appropriate stairways add color and visual interest.

At the University of Pennsylvania, William Penn's coat of arms is combined with contemporary lettering and detailing on slim steel pylons to identify campus buildings that are designed in divergent architectural styles.

Inside dormitories, slate panels and chalk are incorporated with room identification; students can leave messages without leaving a mess.

Marking passages
Celebrating events and rites of passage

A 100th anniversary celebration for the New York Public Library looks forward to the next 100 years rather than casting its eye back over the past. To show what the library is and wants to be, and to suggest the range of its collections—which span music, Braille books, historic documents, prints, and electronic media—the design focuses on the word "library" itself, composing it from an assortment of representative letterforms.

Both the word and the initials adorned numerous banners, publications, and a wide variety of commemorative merchandise.

"When you are courting a nice girl, an hour seems like a second. When you sit on a red-hot cinder, a second seems like an hour. That's relativity," explained Albert Einstein.

Perception of time is drawn from our personal perspective. We celebrate an institution's birthday, though it was never "born." We fuss over a 25th anniversary or centennial, imbuing an arbitrary number with meaning borrowed from our human life cycle. When creating designs to mark these passages, we not only acknowledge this human subjectivity, we count on it. We capitalize on the viewer's perspective, experience, and expectations. A twinkle hinting at a candle waiting to be blown out, a juxtaposition of styles that evokes the flow of years—these create an effective visual shorthand. Like Einstein's courtship-and-cinder analogy, we use the known to explore the new, making the familiar fresh.

Anniversaries are occasions to recall where things started and to mark how far things have come. Every five years, posters designed to publicize the anniversary of the popular Mobil Masterpiece Theatre television series cheer the achievements of the long-running program.

To herald the show's 20th anniversary, fragments of highly publicized images from years past are integrated into the text, illustrating the programs that the text is celebrating.

For the 10th year, a cornucopia of titles recalls just a few of its notable contributions to the television schedule.

For the 15th year, 15 candles glow on a traditional birthday cake featuring tiers of books and TV monitors.

"It's all in the numbers."

Numbers are the quickest way to communicate a span of time. Words like "decade," "quarter" or "centennial" seem vague compared to the precision and impact of an exact count.

The red "o" of the Mobil logo becomes a zero in the "10" to celebrate the anniversary of Mobil's sponsorship.

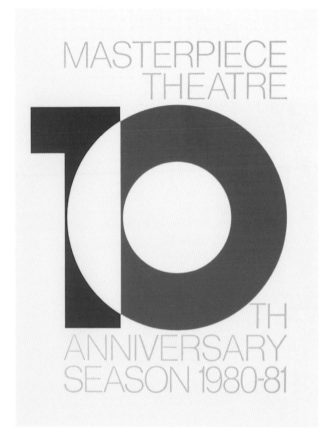

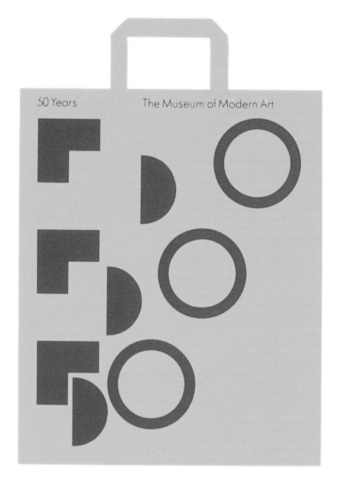

An artistic interpretation of the figure 50 animates an anniversary shopping bag for the Museum of Modern Art.

Best Products' 25th year mark suggests turning a new leaf on the calendar.

Banners waved across Ahmedabad, India, during the 100th anniversary of Calico Mills, the employer of some 75,000 people there.

The 350th celebration logo for the city of Boston uses minimal graphics to contain two words and an impressively big number.

The "125" for the Albright-Knox Art Gallery features split figures of two typographic styles 125 years apart.

domus

Architettura Design Arte Comunicazione *Architecture Design Art Communication*   Dicembre/December 1999   **821**   Lire 15.000   7.75

domus

Architettura Design Arte Comunicazione *Architecture Design Art Communication*   Gennaio/*January* 2000 **822** Lire 15.000 € 7.75

The turn of the millennium offered design possibilities that don't come around very often. (Once every 1,000 years, to be exact.) To make the most of the milestone, the monthly magazine *Domus* commissioned two cover designs as bookmarks before and after the event.

The first, for the December 1999 issue, features fragments of iconic works of 20th-century artists, architects, and designers: a piece of a Calder mobile, a sliver of a Macintosh chair, a slice of a Picasso painting, a glimpse of Frank Lloyd Wright's "Falling Water."

The second cover, for the January 2000 issue, uses the same format to survey some of the problems we will face in the 21st century: water and air pollution, loss of habitat, fossil fuel depletion, the extinction of endangered species, overpopulation, droughts, famines, and a host of other concerns.

Loving cups and statuettes are all well and good, but awards don't have to be trophies or figurines that gather dust on the mantelpiece.

In ancient times, a laurel wreath crowned triumphant athletes. This modern interpretation of such a crown, made of polished brass, was given to the winners of the Mobil Grand Prix track and field competitions.

The Kennedy Center Honors are awards designed to be seen on television during the annual broadcast of the ceremony. The awards themselves are bright and colorful, and meant to be worn with formal attire.

KENNEDY CENTER HONOR

RICHARD RODGERS

DECEMBER 3, 1978

The holiday season keeps coming 'round, year after year. It's always a challenge to find new ways to herald it and welcome the event. Any transformation that remakes the familiar holiday symbols is worth pursuing.

For a card celebrating Christmas, Hannukah, and New Years, two attached, movable triangles become a dial-yourself-a-wish card, as well as a hangable tree ornament.

Scorch marks add a light-hearted and unexpected wink to the red and green flames of this Christmas card.

For Marlin, Christmas snow-flakes are formed from the company's razor blades, themselves sharp and shiny as ornaments.

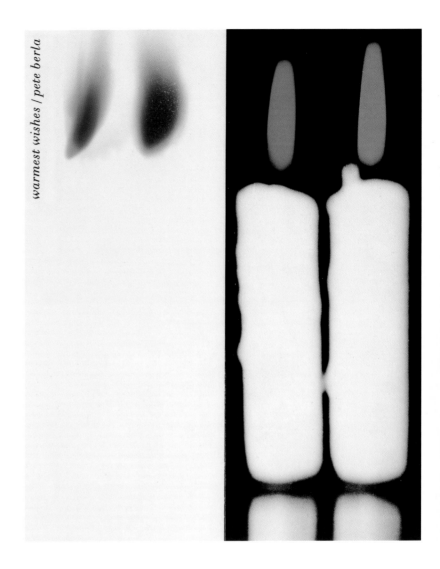

warmest wishes / pete berla

Merry Christmas from

MARLIN

Marlin Firearms Co.   Razor Blade Division

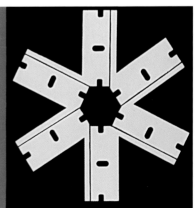

TO SASHA CHERMAYEFF, PHILIP & PHINEAS HOWIE, SEPT. 17, 7 LBS. 11.5 OZ.
LIVIA

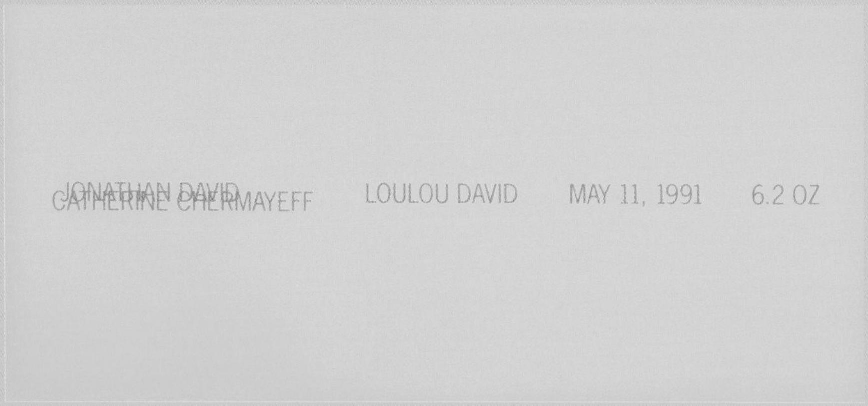

JONATHAN DAVID
CATHERINE CHERMAYEFF   LOULOU DAVID   MAY 11, 1991   6.2 OZ

PHINEAS ALEXANDER HOWIE

AUGUST 28 1992

8 LBS. 9OZ.

SASHA CHERMAYEFF & PHILIP HOWIE

FANNY
CATHERINE ˅ JONATHAN LOULOU ˄ DAVID
CHERMAYEFF   12:46PM
FEBRUARY 7
1993
6LB 6OZ

Births, deaths, marriages, graduations, and commencements—all are important turning points worth noting. They also are design opportunities worth taking advantage of.

Commemorating almost any event is an excuse to make typographic observations or to revisit and reinvent clichés.

One hundred matches, with 50 of them burned to varying degrees, mark a birthday.

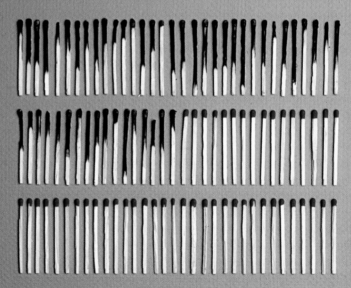

Creating landmarks
Making places memorable

Gertrude Stein's well-worn description of Oakland, California—"There's no there there"—is overused…but for good reason. It touches on the sense of place that grounds us, that links us to our surroundings, that distinguishes one landscape from another (or fails to, in Stein's eyes). Environmental graphics can play a role in forging that sense of identity. They can evoke a "there there."

Some sites, of course, already have a distinctive and powerful personality long before the designers wander onto the scene. In these cases, design can reflect the materials, tones, or images that characterize a specific location. Other, newer places may have no established iconography of their own; so it is up to the designer to establish them, using the site's activities or role or the population it serves as a starting point.

The office tower at 9 West 57th Street in New York City is a giant ski slope of a building designed by Skidmore, Owings & Merrill. A huge red 9 sitting on the sidewalk in front appears to have come sliding down the facade—despite the fact that the great digit weighs many tons (constructed of half-inch plate steel) and is ten feet high and five feet thick. The building's owner pays annual rent for the 9, which sits on city property. In a very real sense, then, the novel numeral has become much more than the address of a destination. It is a destination itself, a frequent backdrop for tourist photos and fashion shoots on this busy, exclusive shopping street.

The success of the 9 as a landmark led to a playful name for the building's lower-level restaurant: 8½.

The starting point for designing an identification sign is its sightlines and audience: Where will it be seen from? Who will see it? For freestanding identification, a vertical format allows maximum size and visibility with a minimal footprint.

At the St. Louis Children's Zoo, a tower of building blocks spiraling into the air marks the entrance.

The Hudson River Museum sign is a slab of steel cut to suggest the irregular shoreline of the river.

A 150-foot-tall pylon along the main highway south of Richmond, Virginia, marks a Philip Morris plant and visitors' center. It is composed of graphic fragments of the company's famous brands.

Turning Stone is the name of the gaming casino in upstate New York operated by the Oneida Indians of the Iroquois nation. Standing in an open field, the 30-foot "stone" entry sign turns slowly and mysteriously.

"Gene Segment" is the name of a sculpture situated in the entry plaza of a research building at the Mt. Sinai Medical Center in Manhattan. The welded steel is faced with mirror-finish aluminum panels that reflect the sky and clouds above.

A polished stainless steel column marks the headquarters of publisher Harper & Row. Its rounded surface reflects and intensifies the urban setting.

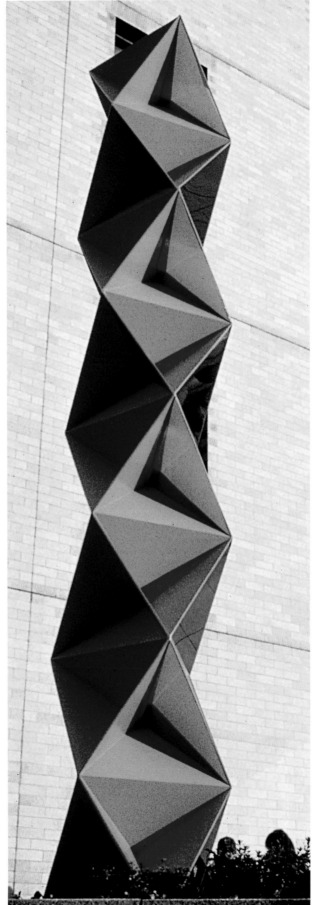

"My home." "My town."
"My community." People naturally
form bonds to their surroundings. How can design create,
or at least reinforce, those
bonds between people and
places? Displaying local crafts-
manship is one way to nurture
pride of ownership.

The tile mural of the Lisbon
Aquarium is on a wall some
five stories high and 240 feet
long. It stretches from outside
the aquarium to the interior
spaces where visitors gather,
meet, buy tickets, and pro-
ceed to the oceanarium itself.

The mural is crafted from
54,000 six-inch-square blue-
and-white tiles, a centuries-old
Portuguese tradition. Images
of fish and other aquatic
animals taken from photographs
were pixilated by computer,
then each pixel was enlarged
to the size of a tile and replaced
by a pattern equivalent to the
pixel's color density. Up to
10 different geometric patterns
were used for each value.

Seen from a distance, the
wall appears to be a series of
photographic images representing sea life. Viewed close
up, the images dissolve,
becoming an abstract tapestry.

A landmark doesn't have to be a single object. It can be an accumulation of visual elements that add up to a memorable visual language. Individually, each part has its own presence and personality. Together, they create a sense of place.

The St. Louis Children's Zoo includes a series of large imaginary animals. The drinking fountain in the lion's mouth lets kids become lion tamers, sticking their heads inside the jaws of the jungle king. It also presents a wonderful photo opportunity.

Nearby, a bird moves with the wind. A red dinosaur grazes on top of a hill, where steam rising from the heating plant below embellishes a fantasy.

Introducing an unusual visual language helps create the equivalent of a new landmark.

Furniture showrooms usually are a sea of desks and chairs, and can be quite boring. In the GF Furniture showroom, cones that rotate when touched are scattered throughout the space, giving a visual cohesiveness and intrigue. The cones, each painted differently, point to key floor samples.

At the headquarters of Digital Computer, lively black and white square aluminum tubes are attached on point to the exterior walls. At first glance, they might appear to be an abstract sculpture. In fact, the tubes spell out the company name in a binary code.

"Can you imagine a building as nice as a hole in the ground?" designer George Nelson once asked. A landmark need not just call attention to what is there. It can evolve over time as it calls attention to what might be there.

What better way to mark the opening of a new theater than to raise a curtain. During the renovation and reconstruction of an old theater near the once infamous intersection of 42nd Street and Broadway, a curtain image rose slowly and teasingly at three-month intervals, eventually revealing the silhouettes of kids forming the letters of the word "victory." The final image, once fully visible, symbolized the intended audience for the reborn New Victory Theater.

The idea for this temporary barricade at a building construction site in Manhattan was to give "sidewalk superintendents" windows through which to monitor the building's progress. The portholes remained in the same position as the barricade was repainted with a different theme every few months to reflect the changing seasons. Here, winter snowmen take the place of bats, witches, carved pumpkins, and other signs of autumn.

Temporary fences at construction sites have long been exploited (remember the time-honored admonition to "Post no Bills"?). But designers see the barricades as a sort of canvas past which vehicles and pedestrians are constantly moving, providing passersby with ever-shifting vantage points.

On Chicago's Michigan Avenue, the famous Playboy bunny is broken up into fragments on protruding fins. The image is quite abstract at first, but suddenly comes into focus as cars or pedestrians pass.

On Madison Avenue in Manhattan, the one-way traffic is treated to a changing spectrum of color and form as it speeds (or crawls) along.

About a block away from the Corcoran Gallery of Art in Washington, D.C., the museum's name suddenly forms. Until that moment of clarity, the banners that spell the name are simply attractive streaks of color mysteriously animating the building with fragments of letters.

Planting a flag is an age-old way to show ownership. Massed banners define an area. Much as lions and wolves define their territories by urinating around the perimeter, people mark property boundaries with banners (a much more sanitary solution).

A changing series of banners attached to lamp-posts delineates the campus of Rockefeller Center. The design suggests the Art Deco spirit of the architecture, reinforcing a distinct sense of place.

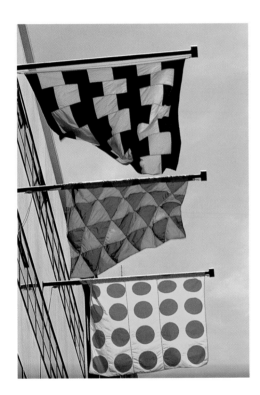

At New York's Museum of Modern Art, the purpose for hanging banners was to draw attention in an artistic way to its mid-block location on West 53rd Street, as well as to announce new exhibitions.

Colorful banners, visible through the glass facade of the main building on the University of Connecticut's downtown Stamford campus, act as identification. They also add a festive, airy feeling to the atrium, helping to open the building's bustle and energy to the otherwise closed off corporate neighborhood.

Representing the nation
Finding new expressions of familiar symbols

"You're a grand old flag," wrote George M. Cohan. "Three cheers for the red, white, and blue," sings the chorus of "Columbia the Gem of the Ocean." Even America's national anthem is named after its banner. From a design viewpoint, clearly, Old Glory is a hugely successful logo—a brand identity to beat the band.

In designs meant to evoke the spirit, politics, or culture of the United States, the familiar pattern of stars and stripes, as well as the red, white, and blue palette, offer a compelling tool. Even a *suggestion* of these elements triggers a cavalcade of associations. The associations and emotions they provoke are different for each individual viewer...which is precisely what makes them so flexible a tool and sparks so personal and powerful a connection.

The official symbol designed for the U.S. bicentennial was a five-pointed star shaped by red, white, and blue ribbon. The elements trigger instant recognition.

The silhouette of an old-fashioned pen point instantly says "graphic arts." The stars and stripes say "U.S.A." The Russian words proclaim "American Graphic Arts," the name of a United States Information Agency exhibition that traveled throughout the Soviet Union during the height of the cold war. The visual elements come together in a way that is simultaneously original and instantly recognizable.

АМЕРИКАНСКАЯ ГРАФИКА

At the Museum of Immigration at Ellis Island in New York Harbor, an undulating flag expresses the interplay between the symbol of the country and the fabric of its people. The flag is made with a series of vertical prisms. As the visitor passes by, the stars and stripes turn into the faces of 1,000 Americans from all ethnic backgrounds.

A "flag" representing American graphic arts (above) is composed of the tools of the graphic artist.

The cover of a catalog about the program "Art in the Embassies" is an abstract expressionistic painting of the stars and stripes. The feeling is fresh and bold and free, the very characteristics that our embassies abroad strive to communicate.

Such is the power of well-known visual themes that they are instantly understood, even after they are fragmented, distorted, cropped, reassembled, and merged with other symbols.

At the United States pavilion at Expo '67 in Montreal, visitors ascended the world's longest escalator to the top of a huge Buckminster Fuller geodesic dome. Along the way, they passed a cloud of fragmented red and white stripes that suggested the American flag.

A five-story-high banner hanging in the transparent dome of the pavilion proclaimed "U.S.A." at a size visible from great distances. Other banners displayed pop art in vogue at that time, including works by Andy Warhol, Jim Dine, and Claes Oldenburg. The angular image is a Fuller geodesic world map realized by Jasper Johns.

A poster for posters. A poster for an exhibition of American posters at the National Museum of American Art includes snippets of paper left over from creating the title as well as the scissors that cut them out. These elements emphasize the mood of directness and immediacy.

In one section of the "A Nation of Nations" exhibition, which was designed and built for the Smithsonian Institution to help celebrate the U.S. bicentennial, political campaign buttons form the flag. Examined individually, the buttons convey the diversity and mix of national origins as reflected in the diverse names of the candidates running for office. Taken together as a single image, the flag is the embodiment of *E Pluribus Unum*, out of many, one.

The flag represents the nation. But so too do countless institutions and artifacts that make up our communities and our culture. They are artifacts of our shared heritage.

The important and valuable idea of the "A Nation of Nations" exhibition, designed and built for the American bicentennial, was to contain visitors by raising the floor and lowering the ceiling along the pathway. This layout enlarged the space for exhibit artifacts and, more importantly, eliminated the need for individual cases to protect the objects. The shift in viewpoint also made it feasible to include very large artifacts from the Smithsonian's vast collection, such as a complete Conestoga wagon.

In the United States, the army and public schools have historically been major forces in assimilating immigrants. To convey this, the exhibition meticulously recreated a World War II army barracks from Fort Dix, New Jersey, and a quintessential 1930s classroom from Cleveland, Ohio.

There are many of ways to represent the nation graphically.

For the American bicentennial exhibit at the Smithsonian Institution a collage crafted from massed immigrant passport photos on this poster suggests the nation's far-flung roots.

If the photo collage is additive, the image on the facing page is subtractive. Removing most of the capital letter "U" in "U.S." takes away two side-by-side rectangles in an evocative homage to the twin towers of the World Trade Center. The hand-cut image appeared on the op-ed page of *The New York Times* soon after September 11.

A Nation of Nations

How best to represent the United States, quickly and visually, to a largely Japanese audience at Expo '70 in Osaka? A display assembled diverse artifacts of American culture, from a forest of folk-art weathervanes and whirligigs to the Apollo 12 space capsule, which had recently landed. Individually, each object spoke only for itself. Collectively, they spoke of America.

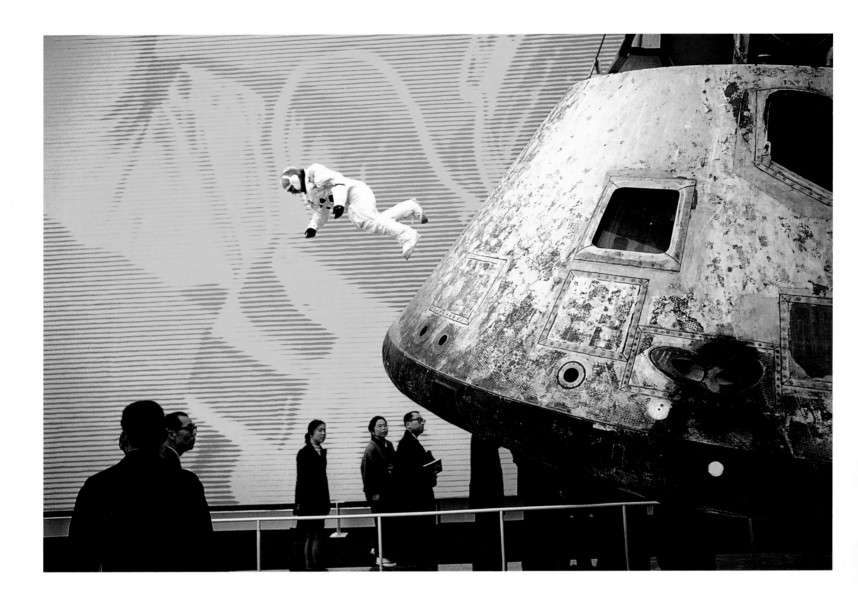

Representing the nation on Mars.

BROWN JOHN CHERMAYEFF
& GEISMAR
235 E 50 ST
NEW YORK 22 NY

Brownpohn (8859)

Brownjohn,Chermayoff & Gerismar.
235 East 50th Street
New York 22, N.Y.

Brownjohn, Shermenzeff & Geismar
235 East 50th St.
New York City

NA009 PD=HOBOKEN NJER 11 833AME=
=MR BROWNJOH, CHERMAYEFF AND GEISMAR=

Brownjohn Chermayoff & Geismar
235 East 50 Street
New York City, NY

Mr. Brownjohn
Brownjohn Chermayess & Geismer
235 East 50 St.
NYC 22

2-36348 Brownjohn Chermayeff & Geismnn 21459
FIRST PROOF—Sept. 14, 1959

BROWNJOHN CHERMAYEFFT& Geismar
235 East 50th St.
New York,N.Y.

Needed by Noon

Brownjohn Chermaye & Geismar
235 East 50th Street
New York, New York

Brown John Chermayeff & Geismar
235 East 50th Street
New York 22, N. Y.

BROWNJOHN, SHERNOYOSS
AND GEISMAR
235 EAST 50TH STREET
NEW YORK CITY

ATT: MR. ROBERT BROWNJOHN

6 21 59 F   T 47 T   20868
BROWN JOHN CHERMAYEFF AND GUESMAN
NEW YORK N Y

Mr. Robert Brownjohn
Ivan Chermayoff
Thomas Geismar
65 W. 56th St.
New York, N. Y.

Brownhohn, Chermayeff & Geismar Company
235 East 50th Street
New York, New York

Geismar & Chermayeff Brownjohn
235 East 50th Street
New York City, New York

Brownjohn, Chermayess & Geismar

ADRESS 235 East 50th Street

New York, 22, N.Y.

M. Geismar

C. Brownjohn & Geismar
235 E. 50th St.
N. Y. City

19. N.

Brownijohn,Chermazeff& Geismar
235 East 50th Street
York,N.Y.

Browngreen, Chermayeff & Geismar
235 E. 50 Street
New York 22, New York

Mr. Ivan Chermayeff
Robert Brownjoh, Ivan Chermayef
and Thomas Geismar
235 East 50th St.
New York, 22
New York

Chermayeff & Geismar Brownjohn
235 East 50th St.
New York, New York

Brownjohn-Shermanzeff & Geismar
235 East 50th St.
New York, N. Y.

Brown, Chermayoff & Geismar
235 East 50 Street
New York City

Brownjohn Chermaydff & Geismar
235 E. 50th Street
New York, N.Y.

BROWNJOHN, HERMAYEFF & GEISMAR
235 East 50th Street
New York City 22, New York

John Brown-Chermayeff-Geismar
235 E. 50th. St.,
New York 22, N. Y.

Mr. T. van Chermayeff
Brownjon, Chermayeff & Geismar
235 East 50th Street
New York City

Office Mgr.
Brownhohn Chermayeff & Geismar
235 E. 50th St.
NY NY

BROWNJOHN CHERMOGEFF & GEISMAR
235 EAST 50TH STREET
NEW YORK , NEW YORK

Brownjohn, Chermayeff &
Gusmar
235 E. 50th St.
New York 22, N.Y.

Brownjohn, Chermayoff & Geismar
235 East 50th Street
New York, N.Y.

..... Brown, John, Chermayeff & Geismar ....
235 E. 50th St.
New York 22, N. Y.

BROWN-JOHN CHERMAYEFF & GEISMAR
235 EAST 50TH ST
NEW YORK 22 N Y
10-59

CHERMAYEFF & GEISMAR BROWN
235 E. 50TH STREET
NEW YORK 22, N. Y.

Mr. Robert Brownjohn
c/o Brownjohn, Geismar & Chermayeff
235 East 50
N.y., N.Y.

BROWNJOHN CHERMAYEFF
235 EAST 50TH ST
NEW YORK CITY

Chermayeff G. Brownjohn
235 East 50th. St.,
New York, N. Y.

Mr. Ivan Chermaieff
Brownjohn, Chermaieff, Geismar
235 East 50th Street
New York, N.Y.

Mr. Thomas Geismar
Brownjohn,Chermayeff & Geismar
235 East 50th Street
New York,N.Y.

Brownjohn - Schermayeff &
Geismar
235 EST
N.Y.C

Brownjohn, Chermayoff & Geismar
235 East 50th Street
New York, N.Y.

Brownjohn, Chermeyeff & Geismar
235 50th St.
New York 22 N.Y.

9/10   :36   SENT TO
COLORCRA
SOLD TO
BROWNJOHN CHERMAYOFF & GEISMAR
ADDRESS
235 EAST 50 ST. N.Y.C

TERMS OF SALE 2% Discount allowed on monthly accounts if paid on or before the tenth of the mon
will be allowed if paid within 30 days from date. No claims allowed after pape

DESCRI

ATTENTION
STATIONERY BUYER

Brownjohn - Shermazeff & Geismar
235 East 50 St

Brownjohn Chermeyeff & Geismar
235 East 50th St.
New York, N. Y.

BROWNJOHN-CHERMAYOFF & GEISMAR
235 EAST 50th STREET
NEW YORK CITY

Passing time
Designing over four decades

The origins of graphic design go back to cave drawings, past clay tablets along the Nile, through illuminated manuscripts and movable type to 19th-century posters and broadsides, and finally to the 20th century, when Modernist design practitioners emerged.

Early pioneers such as Herbert Bayer, A.M. Cassandre, Herbert Matter, Willem Sandberg, Jan Tschichold, and Piet Zwart worked in Europe. The next generation, including Armin Hoffman, Alvin Lustig, Josef Müller-Brockmann, and Paul Rand, worked as individual practitioners on both sides of the Atlantic.

As students of these pioneers, Chermayeff & Geismar was formed in the late 1950s with the idea of taking the new approach to graphic design to another dimension by working collaboratively and in a wider range of disciplines.

While the world has changed greatly, and constantly, over the ensuing years, the work has remained consistent—not in style, but in its approach to design. Accepting the Modernist ideal that design is a problem-solving discipline, Chermayeff & Geismar has sought to humanize that ideal through humor, artistic invention, and an entrepreneurial spirit.

Columbia Records
poster

Book jacket

Wash Up!
packaging

Experimental
typography brochure

+dd
−tract
xultiply
div÷de

f1rst

CIBA sample packages

Book cover

Streetscape, U.S. pavilion,
Brussels World's Fair

Brownjohn, Chermayeff &
Geismar business card

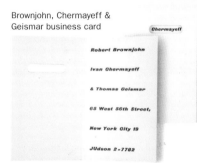

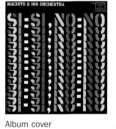

Pepsi-Cola Christmas
display

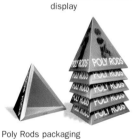

Pepsi-Cola
annual report

Travel agent identity

Album cover

Poly Rods packaging

1957   1958   1959

Robert Brownjohn,
Ivan Chermayeff,
Tom Geismar

1957 Robert Brownjohn, Ivan Chermayeff and Tom Geismar form Brownjohn Chermayeff & Geismar, with office in one room on West 56th Street, NYC ▪ Design record album covers by the dozen for Columbia Records ▪ Design numerous book jackets ▪ Hire first employee, Stanley Eisenman
1958 Move office to three-room suite on East 50th Street ▪ Retained by Pepsi-Cola to design company magazine and displays in lobby of Pepsi's new Park Avenue building ▪ Retained by Howard Wise Gallery to design series of poster announcements ▪ Design graphic "American Streetscape" for U.S. pavilion at Brussels World's Fair
1959 Develop extensive pack-aging lines and graphics for CIBA Pharmaceuticals ▪ Firm's work recognized in early issue of *CA Magazine*, with article "The Bold Young Men". Story in *Graphis* magazine follows

Chase Manhattan Bank
identity

Glade air freshener packaging,
wins "package of the year" award

"That New York"
experimental
typography
brochure

Today and Tomorrow

Museum of
Modern Art
brochure

"Graphic Arts USA"
exhibit in Russia

АМЕРИКАНСКАЯ ГРАФИКА

Museum
of Modern Art
banners

Howard Wise Gallery
announcements

Museum of
Modern Art
book jacket

Print magazine
cover

American
Film Institute
identity

U.S. Information Agency
exhibit

Mobil

Mobil identity

Pepsi-Cola
exhibit poster

GF rotating logo

The Art of the French Poster

An Exhibition at the Pepsi-Cola
World Headquarters, 500 Park Ave.

November 1st through 25th

Xerox brochure

Fortune magazine cover

FORTUNE
500

Torin Corporation
annual report

John F. Kennedy Memorial Library
traveling exhibit

1960 1961 1962 1963 1964

1960 Robert Brownjohn moves to London; firm name changed to Chermayeff & Geismar Associates ▪ Win commission to design identity for newly merged Chase National Bank and Bank of the Manhattan Company ▪ Have firm exhibit at The Composing Room, and develop experimental type project
1961 Commissioned to develop graphic identity and other projects for newly expanded Museum of Modern Art ▪

Move to new offices on East 54th Street
1962 Feature article in *Print* magazine ▪ Commissioned by USIA and AIGA to design major exhibition of U.S. graphic arts to travel throughout Soviet Union
1963 Chermayeff and Geismar become partners in multidisciplinary firm Cambridge Seven Associates ▪ Chermayeff elected president of American Institute of Graphic Arts (AIGA) ▪ Begin decade-long design relationship with Xerox Corporation

1964 Commissioned by Socony Mobil Oil Corp. to develop new identity for Mobil. Beginning of 35-year relationship ▪ Commissioned by Kennedy family to design traveling exhibit to raise funds for proposed presidential library

Tom Geismar
and Ivan Chermayeff

First new-generation Mobil
station, New Haven, CT

Signs for Reston, VA,
first planned town
in U.S.

U.S. pavilion at Expo '67,
Montreal, exhibit

Innovation
magazine cover

St. Louis
Children's Zoo
identification
tower

Architectural Forum
magazine cover

Screen Gems
identity

National Park
Service identity

U.S. Information
Agency poster

Design Media identity

MBTA (Boston)
identity

New England
Aquarium

Poster and identity for
The Electric Circus

Lion fountain,
St. Louis
Children's Zoo

Burlington Industries
annual report

Seatrain
identity

XEROX

Xerox Corporation identity

1965   1966   1967   1968   1969

1965 Chermayeff elected
trustee of Museum of Modern
Art ▪ Boston transit system
unveils new "T" identity and
station graphics
1966 Join with Cambridge
Seven Associates to design all
exhibits for official U.S. pavilion at Expo '67 in Montreal ▪
Commissioned by National
Park Service to develop new
identity ▪ Move to greatly
expanded offices in the Girl
Scouts building on Third Avenue
1968 Ivan Chermayeff and

Henry Wolf cochair Aspen
Design Conference "The Rest
of Our Lives"
1969 Joint venture with architects Davis, Brody and designer
Rudolph deHarak wins USIA
competition to design U.S.
pavilion at Expo '70 in Osaka

Tom Geismar
and Ivan Chermayeff

Ivan Chermayeff
at New York Coliseum
auto show

White House
Conference
on Children

Poster for
productivity
exhibit,
Smithsonian
Institution

A SPECIAL EXHIBIT ON AMERICAN PRODUCTIVITY | IF WE'RE SO GOOD WHY AREN'T WE BETTER? | THE NATIONAL MUSEUM OF HISTORY AND TECHNOLOGY

Pan Am travel posters

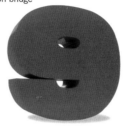

9 West 57th Street
construction bridge

9 West 57th Street
sculpture

Poster for
International
Design Conference,
in Aspen

WAR AND PEACE

Poster for television series

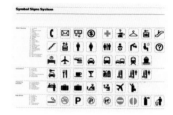

"Symbol Signs" study—
first publication

Claes Oldenburg
catalog

"The Mill" exhibit
Burlington Industries

Menus for first
Pan Am 747 flights

Philip Morris
tower sign

Identity for WGBH,
channel 2, Boston

Garvan Galleries at Yale

This book about the work of Claes Oldenburg was written by Barbara Rose for The Museum of Modern Art

U.S. pavilion, Expo '70,
Osaka, Japan

National
Park Service
sign standards

Owens-Illinois
identity

Poster, American Museum
of Immigration

Idea Book for Xerox

1970   **1971**   **1972**   **1973**   **1974**

Tom Geismar during
installation at Expo '70, Osaka

Tom Geismar and
Ivan Chermayeff

1970 Expo '70 inflated dome
pavilion proves great success
▪ Commissioned by Nixon
administration to develop all
graphics for major White
House Conference on Children
▪ "The Mill" exhibit begins successful 10-year run as major
tourist attraction in midtown
Manhattan
1971 Develop graphics for
inaugural flights of 747 aircraft
and for famous poster series
for Pan Am
1972 Begin decades-long

assignment to design posters
for television shows and cultural
events sponsored by Mobil
1973 Ivan Chermayeff and
Richard Saul Wurman cochair
First Federal Design Assembly
in Washington
1974 Tom Geismar, as
chairman of AIGA/DOT committee, issues report establishing
new national signage standards

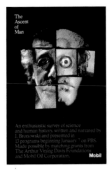
Poster for television
series

Norlin annual report
LP record

Poster for
television show

University of
Pennsylvania campus
sign program

Best Products identity

Subway posters for New York museums

John F. Kennedy
Presidential Library exhibits

Special issue of *Idea*
magazine (Japan)

American Chemical Society
traveling exhibit

Minstrel Man

Designers'
Saturday
poster

EPA
U.S. Environmental
Protection Agency identity

MoMA 50th
anniversary
shopping bag

Guggenheim Museum
poster

GUGGENHEIM
MUSEUM
OPEN FREE TUESDAY
EVENINGS
89th St & 5th Ave
5 to 8 pm
Made possible
by a grant from Mobil

Westvaco calendar,
first year

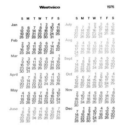

Official
identity for
American
Revolution
bicentennial

Flag wall, IBM World Trade Americas
headquarters

BETWEEN
THE WARS

Reception area
Philip Morris,
Richmond, VA

Poster
for television
series

City at 42nd Street proposal

"A Nation of Nations"
Smithsonian bicentennial exhibit

Koç
Koç Holding identity

1975 1976 1977 1978 1979

Ivan Chermayeff at
IBM World Trade Americas
headquarters

1975 Commissioned to design
the official identity for the U.S.
bicentennial celebration in 1976
▪ Steff Geissbuhler joins firm
as associate
1976 Design for Smithsonian's
major bicentennial exhibition,
"A Nation of Nations," begins
10-year run at National
Museum of American History
1977 After years of false
starts, location of Kennedy
Presidential Library is fixed,
and firm is commissioned to
develop all the exhibits

▪ Develop comprehensive
graphic standards system for
all Environmental Protection
Agency (EPA) publications
1978 Steff Geissbuhler and
John Grady made partners in
the firm ▪ Ivan Chermayeff and
Tom Geismar elected to Alliance
Graphique Internationale (AGI)
▪ Begin a multi-decade relationship as design consultants to
Koç, a major Turkish holding
company
1979 Ivan Chermayeff and
Tom Geismar receive Gold Medal

of the AIGA ▪ Participate in
visionary plan for New York's
42nd Street ▪ Develop logo
and identity graphics for Best
Products catalog showrooms

First American Institute of Graphic Arts "annual"

Embassy identity

Second-generation Mobil stations

Mobil graphic standards

Philip Morris, Cabarrus County, NC, giant quilt

Tishman Speyer, 520 Madison Avenue, construction bridge

Charles Square Hotel identity

CHARLES SQUARE

Louisiana pavilion, '84 World's Fair

Identity for National Aquarium in Baltimore

Philip Morris annual report

Barneys New York identity

Identity for Alvin Ailey Dance Theater

Poster for television program

Poster for Simpson Paper

"The Automobile in Culture" exhibit, Temporary Contemporary (MOCA), Los Angeles

PBS
Public Broadcasting Service identity

"Pride of Place" television series poster

Poster for free evenings at American Museum of Natural History

Identity for the Temporary Contemporary (MOCA), Los Angeles

1980   1981   1982   1983   1984

1980 Firm partners join with Jack Masey and Rusty Russell to form MetaForm Inc. ▪ Special issue of *Idea* magazine entirely devoted to C&G ▪ Steff Geissbuhler elected to Alliance Graphique Internationale (AGI) **1982** Ivan Chermayeff elected to NY Art Directors Hall of Fame **1983** First new generation self-service Mobil stations become operational ▪ Firm moves to new offices on East 26th Street facing Madison Square Park **1984** Firm (with MetaForm)

wins commission for the design of all exhibits at the Statue of Liberty and Ellis Island ▪ Develop "everyman" logo and identity system for PBS, the Public Broadcasting Service

Standing (L–R): Steff Geissbuhler, Tom Geismar, Ivan Chermayeff Seated (L–R): Rusty Russell, Jack Masey, John Grady

Steff Geissbuhler in his office

Right: Tom Geismar at the Statue of Liberty during renovation

ROCKEFELLER
CENTER

Rockefeller Center
identity

Statue of Liberty
exhibit

NY International
Festival of the Arts

"Sequences" poster,
Simpson Paper

THE FIRST
NEW YORK
INTERNATIONAL
FESTIVAL
OF THE ARTS
JUNE 13 – JULY 11
1988

MUSIC, DANCE, THEATRE, OPERA, AND FILM
OF THE 20TH CENTURY

Big Apple Circus
season identity

P E A C E 平和

Peace poster,
Soshin Society

Menu for
The Sea Grill,
Rockefeller
Center

IAAF Mobil
Grand Prix poster
and identity

IAAF
Mobil
Grand Prix
Finale
ISTAF '88

Union Pacific
corporate
brochure

Union Pacific
Corporation

Crane Business
Papers identity

VIACOM FACT SHEET
VIACOM BIOGRAPHY
VIACOM MEMO

Viacom identity

Amicus Journal
cover

Identity for National
Broadcasting Company

NBC

*Designer Engraver
Exchange* for Crane
and ESMA

THE AMICUS JOURNAL

Johnstown Flood Museum

Logan Airport
ice cream parlor

Identity for Univision
television network

1985   1986   1987   1988   1989

1985 Ivan Chermayeff and
Tom Geismar receive Yale Arts
Medal ▪ Geismar receives
Presidential Design Award for
Symbol Sign program ▪ NBC
logo design finally released,
five years after it was designed,
as NBC climbs to No. 1 in
rankings ▪ New identity for
Rockefeller Center unveiled
▪ Steff Geissbuhler elected
first president of NY/AIGA ▪
Firm receives First International
Design Award from Japan Design
Foundation

1986 The Statue of Liberty
Museum opens as part of the
statue's centennial celebration
▪ Increase staff to begin work
on new Ellis Island Immigration
Museum
1988-89 Firm commissioned
to design identities for
major entertainment groups
Time Warner and Viacom

Chermayeff & Geismar staff

Time Warner identity

IBM Multimedia
packaging

Ellis Island
Immigration Museum
exhibit

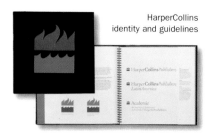

Tennessee Aquarium
identity

Corcoran Gallery
of Art banners

Identity for Artear,
Channel 13, Buenos Aires

Kidpower!
science
playground

Knoll identity
guidelines

Liz Claiborne for Men
packaging

HarperCollins
identity and guidelines

Telemundo
television
network identity

National Public
Radio identity

Identity for
New School
University

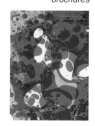

Science City exhibit

Mural at Osaka
Aquarium

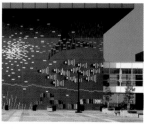

Genoa Aquarium

Merck identity

Symbol Signs

AIGA Symbol Signs

Urban Treehouse at
Children's Museum of
Manhattan

Monadnock
Papers
brochures

Identity for
Hansol Paper, Korea

:Hansol

1990	1991	1992	1993	1994

1990 Ellis Island Immigration Museum opens to national acclaim ▪ Develop identity, exhibits, and exterior murals for new Osaka Aquarium ▪ Liz Claiborne packaging design wins Package of the Year award
1991 Firm name changed to Chermayeff & Geismar Inc. ▪ Ivan Chermayeff and Jane Clark Chermayeff cochair Aspen Design Conference on the subject of children ▪ Begin multiyear relationship with Knoll to reinvigorate graphic identity

▪ United Research becomes Gemini Consulting and commissions extensive identity program and ongoing consultancy
1992 Develop identity and large wall graphics for new Tennessee Aquarium
1993 Selected to redesign all exhibits at the Truman Presidential Library ▪ Steff Geissbuhler elected president of AGI/USA ▪ Develop identities for various Argentine cable and television companies

C&G staff in
open-space office

C&G partners
and associates

New Victory Theater

World of Birds,
Bronx Zoo

Heritage Trails,
Lower Manhattan

New York Public Library,
Rose Gallery exhibit

Irwin Financial
identity

Ads in *Fortune* magazine
and brochure cover for
Gemini Consulting

New 42nd Street identity

Book on American
folk art collection

Freud exhibit, Library of Congress

Andrews McMeel
Universal identity

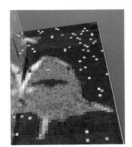
Time Life Medical,
identity and video
packaging

Lisbon Aquarium
tile mural

University of Connecticut
at Stamford identity and
signage program

FactSet
identity

New York
Public Library
centennial logo

SH**O**WTIME

Showtime
cable television
identity

Identity for Eli's Market

Smithsonian Institution
identity

Shinsegai Department Stores,
South Korea, identity

1995   1996   1997   1998   1999

1995 Develop centennial
identity and all related graphics
for New York Public Library
▪ Design series of identities for
international clients in South
Korea, Turkey, Argentina, Japan
1998 Lisbon Oceanarium, with
world's largest tile wall mural,
opens as part of Expo '98 ▪
Tom Geismar elected to NY Art
Directors Hall of Fame
1999 Smithsonian Institution
inaugurates identity system
developed by C&G to tie
together its large network of

museums and research centers
▪ John Grady announces his
retirement ▪ All principals and
associates invited to Mexico
City to conduct conference
and workshop

C&G partners and
associates

Insignia

Insignia identity

National
D-Day Museum

GSA brochure
series

Designing:
book published

**NATIONAL
GEOGRAPHIC**

National Geographic
identity

Chosun Hotel,
South Korea

THE
CHOSUN
HOTEL

Tinicum exhibit

TM
trademark
book
published

Toledo Museum
of Art, identity

Major League
Baseball offices

Overture
identity and
reception
installation

Truman Library
Presidental Galleries exhibit

Identity for
United Nations
Development
Programme

**UN
DP**

arçelik

Identity for
Arçelik, Turkey

Jefferson Library,
Library of Congress

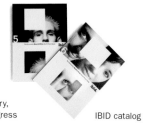

IBID catalog

Atlanta Federal
Reserve Bank
exhibit

2000   **2001**   **2002**   **2003**

L–R: Herman Eberhardt,
Emanuela Frigerio, Tom
Geismar, Ivan Chermayeff,
Steff Geissbuhler, Jonathan
Alger, Keith Helmetag

2000 *TM: Trademarks Designed by Chermayeff & Geismar* published by Princeton Architectural Press and Lars Müller for worldwide distribution ▪ National D-Day Museum, developed with MetaForm, opens in New Orleans. The innovative presentation of personal accounts attracts large crowds ▪ Commissioned to develop extensive new exhibits for Griffith Observatory in Los Angeles ▪ Keith Helmetag and Jonathan Alger named principals of the firm

2001 The Presidential Galleries at the Truman Library open after eight years of development ▪ "D-Day Invasions of the Pacific" exhibit opens at National D-Day Museum ▪ After three-year study, National Geographic approves new graphic identity program

2002 Herman Eberhardt and Emanuela Frigerio named principals of the firm ▪ United Nations Development Programme introduces new identity

2003 Wilburn Bonnell joins firm as a principal ▪ Graphis Press publishes *Designing:*, a book by Ivan Chermayeff, Tom Geismar and Steff Geissbuhler that uses the work of the firm to describe an approach to design that has been consistently applied for over four decades ▪ Exhibition of the firm's work at Cooper Union

Over the years a considerable number of talented people have been members of our office and have contributed in many ways to the designs presented here. Their names are listed with appreciation.

Massimo Acanfora
Richard Amend
Brook Anderson
Lise Andersson
William Anton
Steve Arcella
Anita Ayerbe
Dawn Baird
Eugenia Balcells
Barbara Balch
Judy Ball
Stephen Bamonte
Richard Barnes
Gilda Battude
Bettina Berg
Susan Berman
Kenneth Bess
Olivia Biddle
Weston Bingham
Alice Bissell
Francois Blais
Andres Blanco
Lance Boge
Christopher Borden
Bruce Blackburn
Gail Boyajian
Julia Boynton
Charles Breuel
Edward Broderick
James Broderick
Lisette Buiani
Oscar Buitrago
Andi Schultz-Burnett
Marcus Burnett
Naomi Burstein

Franz Buzawa
Chris Calori
Ken Carbone
Bill Carrig
Hermes German Castañeda
Michael Cervantes
Nicholas Chaparos
Tamara Chinn
Hoi-Ling Chu
Judith Churchill
Emilie Clark
Jennifer Clark
Norman Cloutier
Muriel Convers
Kevin Cornelius
Roberta Cowie
Morris Cymbrowitz
Barbara Daley
Kerry Dantschisch
Margo Davis
Donna DeFeo
Priscilla Deichmann
Walter Deichmann
Diana Deitrich
Edward Deniega
Lisa Derosby
Ellis Dichter
Jay Dillon
Danielle Dimston
Kurt Dittmar
Terry Dobson
Stanley Dornfest
Christopher Douglas
Brandon Downing
Ronald Doyon
Etta Dreskin
Ulysses Drinks
Bart Drury
Fritz Drury
Kim Dunn
Steve Dunne
Frank Dylla

Stanley Eisenman
Laura Eitzen
Judyann Elias
Judith Ellis
David Enoch
Sandra Erickson
Russell Etter
Alison Ewing
Richie Fahey
Chris Farley
Pat Farrell
Peter Felperin
Lorraine Ferguson
Robert Fernandez
Steve Fineberg
Susan Fisher
Anthony Ferrara
Thomas Ferraro
Vernon Ford
Carolyn Foug
Vincent Franco
Steve Frisna
Dirk Fütterer
Robert Fymat
Vincent Gagliostro
Robert Gale
Beau Gardner
Justine Gaxotte
Pamela Geismar
Fabio Gherardi
David Gissen
Sidney Gomberg
Lorentz Gonzalez
Peter Good
Jill Gorelick
Piera Grandesso
Lorelei Grazier
Lori Greenzweig
David Griffing
Henri Gueron
Joseph Guertin
Darrell Gunn

Michael Gutbezahl
Hennelore Hahn
Steve Haines
Madonna Hall
Michael Hanke
Bill Head
Nancy Hechinger
Heiner Hegemann
Karen Hellman
Marnee Henderson
Robert Henry
Steve Herman
Jane Herrick
William Heyer
James Hicks
William Hofer
Timothy Honquest
Matthew Hranek
Cynthia Huggins
Pervinia Hundley
Kenneth Jackson
Shivdasie Jaikaran
John Jay
Steve Jenkins
Oliver Johnson
Eileen Jones
Nina Katchadourian
Melanie Kirchner
Heinz Klinkon
Petra Klusmeyer
George Koizuimi
Stephen Koslowski
Nicoletta Koufos
Audrey Krauss
Julia Krutzel
Barbara Kuhr
Jack Kupiec
Sharon Kupiec
Henricus Kusbiantoro
Samantha Laine
Steve Langerman
Michael Lebron

Jadwiga Lendo
Dominae Leveille
Adrain Levin
Phyllis Levine
Marc Levitt
Karen Lewis
Terry Lewis
Charles Lofton
Stephen Loges
Lou LoMonaco
Michael Loos
Jose Lopez
George Lorenz
Eugenia Lorenzo
Kenneth Love
Richard Lovelace
Larry Lurin
Patsy Madden
Emily Mann
Stephanie Marcus
Fleur Marks
Leonard Marsh
Edward Marson
Robert Matza
Paul May
Mary McBride
Mary McCormick
Diana McHugh
James McKibben
Michael Mensch
Carla Miller
Michele Miller
Cristina Minervini
Lorraine Mintz
Bruce Mohat
Phyllis Montgomery
Eric Moskowitz
Louis Musachio
Susan Muther
Al Nagy
Arthur Natale
Emily Neuman

Adrian Nivola
John Noneman
Charlotte Noruzi
Sean Oakes
Michele O'Brien
Derrick Odom
Constance Old
John Olson
Lea Otten-Profumo
Dan Ouellette
Richard Paccione
Fred Paganini
Donna Pascal
Jane Pasquier
Nancy Paule
Stanley Pearlstein
Jennifer Peerless
Jamie Peloquin
Ben Perez
Ian Perkins
Daniela Perry
Santiago Piedrafita
Scott Plunkett
Johnny Powell
Linda Post
Evelyn Powers
Mary Quinn
Constantine Raitzky
Elizabeth Reed
Angela Reeves
Nancy Register
Suzanne Resnick
Erick Rizzotto
Gerald Robinson
Robert Rodrigues
Susan Rogers
Dorcas Roehrs
Brendan Rooney
Elaine Rooney
Christopher Rose
Erich Rose
Jill Rossi

Mark Rossi
Chris Rover
Lydia Rubio
Deborah Rubstein
Chuck Rudy
Gina Russell
Roger Sands
James Sauter
Kevin Sayama
Cathy Schaefer
Ingo Scharrenbroich
Thomas Schneider
Susan Schunick
Tamara Schwartz
Dorothy Schuster
Louis Scrima
Jose Segura
Deborah Seidman
Eli Sela
Eugene Sercander
Marcus Shaffer
George Shakespear
Haggai Shamir
Adam Shanosky
Mary Shapiro
Lytle Shaw
Lori Shepard
Mitchell Shostak
Alan Shortall
Itaal Shur
Amy Siegel
Joseph Simons
Christianne Smith
Pamela Smith
Bill Sontag
Jane Specter
Irving Springer
Anna Steck
Henry Steiner
Kirsten Steinorth
Christoph Stettler
Gary Stilovich

Greg Strzempka
Sarah Sturtevant
Cindy Suffoletto
Christina Sun
Takuyo Takahashi
Jane Taylor
Dolores Tesch
Michael Tesch
Lou Theoharides
Margaret Thompson
Susan Thornton-Rogers
Deirdre Torney
Paul Trapido
Christina Trimble
Anthony Tsirantonakis
Michael Tudor
Kathleen Tufaro
Charles Unger
Julia Unger
Lou Vallejo
Roger Van den Bergh
Judith Vannais
Lillian Vassallo
Lu Vega
Michael Von Uchtrup
Julie Walsh
Terri Wargo
Claudia Warrak
Thomasina Webb
Bill Weller
Lori Whaley
Diana Wheaton
Pamela White
Gary Whitney
Arlynne Whittingham
Tori Wilke
Anthony Williams
Fred Witzig
Brad Woodworth
Wilson Wright III
Brian Wu
Karen Yamauchi

Alex Yampolsky
Robert Yeo
James Yestadt
Robert Ziering

Interns:
Christian Butte
Adriana Casteñeda
Kenny Chen
So-Hee Cheong
Meg Dreyer
Matthew Gill
Whitney Grant
Evelyn Hafferty
Roland John
Toby Kollman
Jorgine Lee
Jitnadda Lohavichan
Zeynep Oguz
Corina Putz
Gabriele Schies
Sybille Schneider
Lucia Sumarijanto
Suzanne Weiss
Rahel Witschi
Nadine Woerz

We would like to acknowledge the many photographers and illustrators who have contributed their talents to the projects of Chermayeff & Geismar.

Peter Aaron
Tom Allen
David Arky
Ovak Arslanian
R.O. Blechman
Steve Brosnahan
Sally Anderson-Bruce
Marcus Burnett
Seymour Chwast

Paul Davis
Brandon Downing
Eliot Erwitt
Esto
Richie Fahey
Scott Frances
Len Gittlemen
Jeff Goldberg
Barry Halkin
Dave Hoffman
Elliot Kaufman
Jennifer Krogh
Saul Leiter
Jonathan Levine
Maxwell MacKenzie
Jay Maisel
Bard Martin
Peter Mauss
Norman McGrath
James McMullan
Peter Olson
Robert Andrew Parker
Gil Peress
Ann Raymo
William Rivelli
François Robert
Steve Rosenthal
Sebastiao Salgado
Daniel Schwartz
Charles Shorre
Alan Shorthall
Burt Silverman
Rodney Smith
David Sunderberg
Burk Uzzle
Stephan Van Dam
Camille Vickers
James Victore
Bill White
Kevin Woest
Henry Wolf
Karen Yamauchi

We would like to particularly acknowledge the long-term support of:

American Republic Insurance
Cambridge Seven Associates
Chermayeff, Sollogub and Poole, Inc.
Conservation Trust of Puerto Rico
Crane & Co.
May Department Stores
Mobil Oil Corporation
National Aquarium in Baltimore
Philip Morris Companies
David Teiger
Tishman-Speyer
Torrington Manufacturing
United States Information Agency
Jack Masey, Design Director for Expo '67 and Expo '70

We would like to acknowledge the institutions, corporations and individuals who engaged us to help with some of their communications needs:

ABC
Abraham & Strauss Department Stores
Active Aging Association, Tokyo
Adage
Albright-Knox Art Gallery
Alliance for Downtown New York
David Altshuler
Alvin Ailey Dance Theater
Stephen E. Ambrose
American Academy in Rome
American Center for Productivity
American Century
American Chemical Society
American Cinema Editors
American Express Life Insurance
American Film Institute
American Institute of Graphic Arts
American Museum of Natural History
American Paper Institute
American Revolution Bicentennial Commission
Amicus Journal
Andrews McMeel Universal
Andrus Children's Center
Architectural and Engineering News
Artear Argentina
Atlantic Monthly
N.W. Ayer
Banco de Bogotá
Banco de Italia
Edward Larrabee Barnes

Barneys New York
Barrow Street
Basketball Hall of Fame
Beaunit Corporation
Herbert Beckhard
Xavier Bermudez
Best Products Company
Beyer Blinder Belle
BFGoodrich Company
William Bidwell
The Big Apple Circus
Paul Binder
Birmingham Museum of Art
Peter Blake
Joaquin Blaya
Mamdouha S. Bobst
Bond Market Association
Daniel J. Boorstin
David Boorstin
Peter Borelli
Francis Bouyges
Brentano's
David Bright
British Leyland Motors
Bronx Zoo
Brooklyn Botanical Garden
Broward County Library
Brown University
Richard Burkert
Burlington Mills
Butler Rogers Baskett
Aaron Burns
Cable Health Network
Cablevision
Ralph Caplan
Cora Cahan
CARE International
Carnegie Hall
CBS Cable
Center for Addiction and Substance Abuse
Center for Jewish History

Centro de Convensiones de Cartagena
Irene Chambers
Champion Papers
Charles H. Yalem Children's Zoo
Charles Square Hotel
Charter New York
Chase Manhattan Bank
Chickamauga Battlefield
Children's Museum of Manhattan
Chosun Hotel
Joon Chung
CIBA
City of Boston
Clay Adams, Inc.
Cluett, Peabody & Co.
Columbia Records
Columbia University, School of Journalism
Composing Room
Compri Hotels
Con Edison of New York
Conrad Hotels
Container Corporation of America
Continental Anchor Engraving
Corcoran Gallery of Art
Crafton Graphic Company
Crane & Co.
Cummins Engines
Dana Alliance for Brain Initiatives
Davis Brody Bond Architects
Lewis Davis
Myrna Davis
Charles Dayton
Desert Ranch
Design Media
David Deutch
Dictaphone Corporation
Digital Computer

Dime Savings Bank of New York
Diners Club
Directional Industries
Domus Magazine
E.B. Eddy Paper
Edgewood Furniture
Edward S. Gordon Company
Alvin Eisenman
Electric Circus
Eli's Manhattan
Charles Ellis
Ellis Island Immigration Museum
Elmer Holmes Bobst Library
Embassy Communications
Empire Insurance
Endicott Visitor Center
Engraved Stationery Manufacturers Association
Ethical Culture Fieldston Schools
FactSet Research Systems
Marilyn Farley
David C. Farrell
Federal Reserve Bank of Atlanta
FEED Magazine
Festival of India
First Bank System
First New York International Festival of the Arts
Len Fogge
James K. Fogleman
Fortune Magazine
Fort Worth Art Museum
Fox & Fowle Architects
Fox Theaters
Foxboro Stadium
Stephanie French
Alan Friedman
Steve Frykholm
GF Furniture

Gannett/USA Today
Gemini Consulting
General Services Administration
Genoa Aquarium
Geo. J. Ball
Georgia O'Keeffe Museum
Vince Gleason
Clifford Goldsmith
Stanley Goodman
Gramavision
Greenhill & Company
Greenwich Research
Grey Advertising
Grey Entertainment and Media
Griffith Observatory
Griphon
Larry Hackman
Hakuhodo Brand Design
Halaby International
    Corporation
Hansol Paper
Harcourt, Brace, Jovanovich
Hardy Holzman Pfeiffer
    Associates
Tom Hardy
Harper & Row
Harper's Magazine
Harry S. Truman
    Presidential Library
Hastings Creative Arts Council
Hear US
Hechinger Company
John Hechinger
Hecht Company
Heritage Trails
Herman Miller Furniture
Heyman Properties
Carolyn Hightower
Hillier Architects
Jack Hough
Houghton Mifflin Publishers
Hudson River Museum

Hypertherm
IBM
Ibex Wear
Ibid.
Illinois National Bank
Indian Head
Infineer
Insignia
Integrated Living Communities
International Design
    Conference in Aspen
Irwin Financial Corporation
Jack Morton Productions
Jacob's Pillow Dance Company
Japanese American
    National Museum
John F. Kennedy Library
John Hancock Building
John Heinz National Wildlife
    Refuge at Tinicum
Johnstown Flood Museum
Richard Kaplan
Katonah Museum of Art
Kaufman's Department Store
Kennedy Center Honors
Richard Kerans
Kidscommons
George Klein
Kliment & Halsband Architects
Steven Kliment
Knapp Shoes
Knoll Furniture
Koç Holdings
Rahmi M. Koç
Kohn Pederson Fox
Richard Koshalek
La Universal Insurance
Earle E. Layman
Leucadia
Levin & Associates Architects
Library of Congress
Lincoln Center Film Society

Leo Lionni
Liz Claiborne
Los Angeles Public Library
Ludica Magazine
Lykes Corporation
Maguire Thomas Partners
Maio & Co.
Major League Baseball
Manufacturers Hanover Trust
Marcel Breuer Associates
Marriott Hotels
Massachusetts Bay
    Transportation Authority
Maxman Architects
May Department
    Stores Company
Mead Paper
MeadeWestvaco
Merck
Metropolitan Boston
    Transit System
Metropolitan Transit Authority
Frank Metz
Miami International
    Airport Hotel
Fran Michelman
Midsouth Rail
Mico Miller
Will Miller
The Minneapolis Insitute
    of Arts
Mississippi State
    Historical Museum
Monadnock Paper
Morgan Stanley
Mount Sinai Medical Center
Multicanal Argentina
Municipal Art Society
Museum of Contemporary Art
    Los Angeles
Museum of Modern Art
William Myers

NBC
Motoo Nakanishi
Nashua
National Building Museum
National Credit Bank of Russia
National D-Day Museum
National Endowment
    for the Arts
National Fish and Wildlife
    Foundation
National Heritage Board
    of Singapore
National Geographic Society
National Museum
    of American History
National Park Service
National Public Radio
New Bedford Aquarium
New England Aquarium
New 42nd Street
New School University
New Victory Theater
New York and International
    Olympic Committee
New York Art Directors Club
New York Botanical Garden
New York City Department
    of Cultural Affairs
New York City
    Parks & Recreation
New York City Police
    Department
New York Festival of the Arts
New York Hall of Science
New-York Historical Society
New York Philharmonic
New York Public Library
New York State Museum
New York State Urban
    Development Corporation
New York University
New York Times

Nippon Life Insurance
Norlin Corporation
Oceanário de Lisboa
Ohio Center
Old Chatham
    Sheepherding Company
Osaka Aquarium
Overture
Owens-Illinois
PaineWebber
Pan Am
PAOS
I.M. Pei and Partners
Pei Coff Freed & Partners
Pepsi-Cola
Peter Gisolfi Associates
Perkin-Elmer Corporation
Philip Morris Companies
Pilobolus Dance Company
Charles Platt
Poets House
Port Authority of New York
    and New Jersey
Portfolio Center
Watson Powell
Preservation League
    of New York State
Prospect Park Alliance
PBS
Public Spaces NYC
Chris Pullman
Queens Museum
Realty Hotels
Request Television
Restaurant Associates
Hank Richardson
Ring of Fire Aquarium
Rio Algom Corporation
Robert F. Kennedy Foundation
David Rockefeller
Rockefeller Center
The Rockefeller Foundation

Jonathan Rose
Gary Roth
Royal Shakespeare Company
Sandra Ruch
Saks Fifth Avenue
John Sanders
School of Visual Arts
Screen Gems
Scripps Howard
Seatrain Lines
Martin Segal
Herbert Schmertz
Gerald Schneiderman
Shearson-Hamill
Chris Sheppard
Shinsegae Department Stores
Showtime Networks
Simon & Schuster
Simpson Paper Company
Skidmore Owings & Merrill
Smithsonian Institution
Richard Solomon
Sheldon H. Solow
Sony Entertainment
Soshin Society
St. Joe Company
St. Louis Children's Zoo
State of Louisiana
Charles Stendig
George Stevens
Norton Stevens
Rufus Stillman
Inju Sturgeon
Telemundo Television Network
Tempozan Marketplace
Tennessee Aquarium
Thaibok Fabrics
Mary Ann Tighe
TIAA/CREF
Time-Life Medical
Time Warner
Tokio Marine

Toledo Museum of Art
Torin Corporation
Towers Perrin
Translation Magazine
Richard Tucker
Tultex
Tupperware Corporation
Turning Stone Casino
Uarco, Inc.
Union Pacific Corporation
United Banks of Colorado
United Nations Development
    Programme
United Research
United States Department
    of the Interior
USAID
U.S. Department
    of Transportation
U.S. Environmental
    Protection Agency
U.S. Fish and Wildlife Service
United States
    Information Agency
United Technologies
University Club of New York
University of California
    Los Angeles
University of Connecticut
    at Stamford
University of Maryland
    in Baltimore
University of Pennsylvania
Univision Television Network
Van Cliburn Piano Competition
Venture Stores
Viacom
Voice of America
Rawleigh Warner
George Weissman
Weltspartag Sparkasse
Westinghouse

WGBH Boston
Wildlife Conservation Society
White House Conference
    on Children
Whitney Museum of
    American Art
Andrew Wilson
Howard Wise
Women's Rights National
    Historical Park
World Policy Journal
Wrangler Brand (Europe)
Xerox Corporation
Yale University
Young Audiences

gratifying delighting understanding familiarizing adding reducing transforming sequencing foreing accepting flattering talking preparing memorizing subtracting connecting gratifying ripping sequen finding demystifying enjoying starting reinterpreting representing preparing voicing visualizing memorizing